The Gift of
Disappointment

Leilah I. Sampson

The Gift of Disappointment

© 2016 by Leilah I. Sampson

ALL RIGHTS RESERVED.

*"Your Joy is your Sorrow unmasked
And the selfsame well from which
your laughter rises was often times
filled with your tears.
And how else can it be?
The deeper that Sorrow
carved into your being,
the more Joy you can contain."*

~KAHLIL GIBRAN

Foreword

Dear Leilah Iman,

"Beloved child, you are the light of the world. Beloved child, go out spread light to the world. Be strong, be kind, be brave. Know your mine. Know that you're divine. Know that it's alright to be afraid."
~Jai Jagdeesh song *In Dreams*

I first met you, deep inside the darkness so long ago. Deep inside those depths you were inside the womb of the divine mother. Inside the dark fertilizations that was needed. It was meant for a long incubation period but you didn't know it at the time. Your radiant light, your healing and hope for the world and your next perfect kidney, Phil, was waiting for you. You didn't know this. However, it was those very seeds of faith, hope, strength and courage always pulling you forward deep inside that dark womb. There were core patterns you had to break free from. You had the sacred task of building a life of abundance, purification, and needed to strengthen your ability to receive. There were so many gifts waiting for you in 2015 and beyond. You needed to open up, soften and receive them. You did this, all of this, dear Leilah.

It has been my humble honor to support, witness, validate and believe in you during that long incubation, deep inside the darkness. You allowed my support, love and healing messages to penetrate that darkness in order to allow the light of your radiant self, *inside*. Your heart always intuitively leaned into those beams of light. We didn't have to teach your heart this, it just knew.

Just like a new seedling knows how to stretch and reach the sunlight, your heart slowly marinated and integrated all the healing and hopeful messages around you all in divine timing so you could bravely burst forward on that sacred day: December 15, 2015.

I await all the luscious unfolding of divine abundance as your story continues. I believe in you, dear-heart; I knew you would always be where you are, inside the authentic truth of your vast amazing life.

Thank you, and Blessings always,
Monica T. Hagerty, LCSW/Energy Healer

Dedicated to:

To the man who sacrificed his life
and my story can continue to be written.
To his family, I pray this
brings you comfort and peace.
Leilah & Phil

Disappointment is not to your detriment.

TEARS FELL FROM MY EYES DURING MY GAS-GUZZLING, one-hour drive to Jamba Juice. I'd make this drive every day after I came out of the coma. I'm not sure if it was the smoothies or the need to get back into the world and out of solitude that was my addiction after the coma. OK, it probably was both, because let's face it: those smoothies are amazing. These tears were different. Have you ever been so grateful for life, the only emotion you can muster up is an ugly, happy-cry? I parked in my usual spot between two cars and called my older sister. She could hear the sobs and said "Baby those are happy tears."

In 2008, at the age of 19, I was attending the historic Tuskegee University at the bottom of scorching Alabama. Tuskegee University, formally known as Tuskegee Institute, is a part of a collection of Historically Black Colleges and Universities (HBCUs). The city of Tuskegee is not only important in African-American culture, but also in Aviation history, as the area is home to the legendary Tuskegee Airmen. They were the first African-American military pilots who fought in WWII. Tuskegee continues to excel in Aerospace Science Engineering, Chemical Engineering, and but not limited to graduating the nation's top Veterinarians of all ethnicities. My sophomore year there ended before it began. While switching classes on the first day of the new semester; I received a phone call from an unknown number.

"Hello?" I answered reluctantly.

"Hi, may I speak with Ms. Sampson?" a strong male voice asked.

"This is she; may I ask who's calling?" I responded.

"Yes, this is Dr. Bad News Bob. We received your test results and would like you to come to my office here in town," he said with a sense of urgency in his voice.

In my mind, I recalled the 24-hour urine-collection test I had returned the week prior. I'd been having some swelling in my feet, making it painful to walk. I showed my coworkers at the restaurant I waitressed at and they were in shock at the sight of seeing the top of my foot bulge through the straps that crisscrossed it. We all assumed I was just standing on my feet too much, not to mention giving prospective students and their families tours every week as a campus tour guide.

I explained to him, "Sir, I'm a student at Tuskegee and it's the first day of classes. I'm in between classes. How late is your office open? Maybe I can come afterwards or another day because I have to work later."

Dismissing everything I'd just said, he said, "No, I need you to come in now," with more urgency in his voice

I was a little worried at that point.

"Okay, I'm on my way there now. Thank you," I said

He explained how to get there and followed with the address.

Luckily, the office wasn't too far from campus. I figured I'd run to the doctor's office really quick between classes and make it back in time for my next class. Driving to the doctor's office, a million thoughts ran through my head but nothing could've prepared me for the news I was about to receive. It would change my life forever. I remember walking into now what I realize was a Dialysis Clinic. I signed in and nervously waited in the waiting room alone to see the doctor. I thumbed through the many pamphlets on the table that described "Kidney Disease" and how to manage it. It might as well have been written in another language because I didn't understand it or how any of it applied to me. You ever been to a place so unfamiliar that it's like a twilight zone? You're there physically, but not really present. Yeah, that was me in that moment: just a ball of confusion, nervousness, and pressed to finish the first school day. I didn't wait long before a nurse came to get me from the waiting room and escorted me to a small consultation room with just two chairs, a computer, and a sink. I took a seat next to the computer and anxiously waited. Dr. Bad News Bob came in. He was a Caucasian, older male, and looked about in his mid-60s. He was wearing a white coat with hair to match and stethoscope, holding a stack of papers. He explained to me that my lab results were in and the results were "not good." He was explaining something about creatinine and kidney function. He sounded like the teacher from Charlie Brown: all I heard was "whomp, wha, whomp, wha, whomp."

With a blank stare, I kept asking him, "What does all of this mean?"

He proceeded to pull out another sheet of paper that showed a list of about 7-10 possible Kidney Diseases I could have. I began to cry hysterically and refused to believe what he was telling me.

"Wait. Are you sure you have the right patient?" I asked.

He looked to the top of the chart to verify my name and birthday and concluded,

"Yes, Ms. Sampson, these are your results."

"Can we repeat the tests?" I asked, looking up from my hands, wiping my eyes and nose that were running like a faucet.

"I'm sorry, but coupled with the blood work, the 24-hour urine collection is the most accurate test we have," he assured me.

He continued informing me that I would need a Kidney Biopsy to further confirm and specifically diagnose the illness. He pulled out another sheet of paper and slid it to me across the counter; on the list were diseases like Lupus and FSGS. The only one I recognized was Lupus, and I knew that was one of the worst diseases a person could have. I recalled that people with Lupus didn't live very long. I explained to him I was all alone and without any family in Alabama. He advised I call my parents because this matter was urgent. I needed to seek medical attention almost immediately to diagnose what specific disease I had. Early detection is key in controlling and managing any illness.

I left the office, got in my car, and called my dad to explain to him the news I received. He's been a registered nurse for over 15 years, so he understood the lab results better than I did. He understood the severity of the diagnosis.

Sobbing, I said, "Dad, remember the swelling I've been having? Well, I just left the doctor's office and he showed me my test results."

"Okay ... What did he say baby?" dad asked.

Dads always have a way of comforting their little girls with a certain tone and with one word all is made right again. However, in this moment *Dad Magic* wouldn't make this one right.

"He was saying something about kidney numbers, creatinine, and proteins. Dad, what does all of this mean?" I managed to get out between sobs.

Putting on his nursing cap (that he actually never takes off) he said, "It means something is going on with your kidneys. And it could be very serious. We need to get you back home to Chicago and to a hospital here to find out why you're spilling so much protein in your urine. That's the cause of your swelling baby."

"But dad, it's the first day of classes. We just got all the financial aid stuff squared away for me to start the semester."

Much like Dr. Bad News Bob, the seriousness in his voice grew with every word, followed by slight panic.

"Go back to your apartment, pack as much stuff as you can in a carry-on suitcase. I'm booking you a flight out of Atlanta (Hartsfield- Jackson Airport). Leave your car and ask one of your friends to drive you there. You have three hours. Call me before you board."

"Okay, daddy." Followed by machine gun bursts of tears.

I then called my mom at work and told her the news. Like any mother, she was in disbelief.

"Thank you for calling Midway Dental, how may I help you?" the receptionist answered.

"Hey, it's Leilah, Lori's daughter. I need to speak with her. It's very important," I said.

"She may be with a patient, but let me go see. Hold one moment," she said.

"Hey, Leilah! What did the doctor say?" she asked.

"Hey mom, it's not good. I called Dad and explained to him what the results meant and he's booking me a ticket home," I said.

"Wow. What do you mean?" she asked in disbelief.

"Mom, I'm not sure what these numbers mean, but apparently it's serious. Something could be wrong with my kidneys."

"Wow. Are you serious? I just ... I can't...." she responded, trying to make sense of it all.

I drove back to campus where I ran into my best friend

Reggie. Since I'd started crying, my face immediately had begun to swell. I was almost unrecognizable. He was surprised to see my face so swollen so I couldn't avoid telling him the awful news. He too was in utter disbelief and asked, "Baby, what happened to your face?"

"I just left the doctor in town and he explained, there might be something wrong with my kidneys. That's what's causing all of the swelling," I said as I showed him my legs underneath the wide-leg pants I had worn in 100-degree weather.

He hugged me tightly, kissed me on the cheek, told me to make sure I kept in touch, and wished me well. Next, I stopped by the office of a very good mentor and supervisor of the Campus Tour Guide program. I broke the news to her, cried even more, and she reassured me she would handle all of my affairs. She withdrew me from my classes, spoke with financial aid, and tied up any remaining loose ends to ensure I was no longer a student at Tuskegee University.

I called my roommate, Courtney and told her the news. We cried so much that I had to wear sunglasses the rest of the day because of the amount of swelling in my face. My eyes were almost swollen shut. My feet were so swollen they could barely fit in my shoes. The swelling in my feet was unbearable.

I asked her to drive me to the airport. Hartsfield-Jackson Airport is the closest major airport to Tuskegee, at less than two hours away. We arrived at the airport, hugged, and I asked her to take good care of my car while I was gone. I walked into the airport with my carry-on suitcase, leaving my car, apartment, job and school life behind. I approached the TSA checkpoint I was asked to remove my sunglasses to verify I was the same person on my ID. I removed my sunglasses and judging by the shock on the agent's face I immediately began explaining that I had a health condition that caused my face to swell. I didn't even know what I had at that moment, so I was hoping he would let me through without asking any further questions. I breathed a sigh of relief as he let me through without a hassle. I proceeded to the gate and boarded the plane. This was the beginning of the end of my so-called "normal" life. As I flew home gazing out of the tiny plane window, I reflected on the news I'd just received some three hours earlier. I had no idea what was in store for me. It all felt like a terrible nightmare I couldn't wake up from. I knew I needed to go home and face this head-on. I had to do what was best for my health. Judging by the doctor's urgency for me to come into his office during the middle of a school day, I knew it had to be serious.

I arrived home in Chicago and would only return to Tuskegee to gather my things and car. I have many regrets about not completing my bachelor's degree. I felt like I had found my place there at Tuskegee. I was doing well in school, working, and enjoying meeting new prospective students and their families. I enjoyed feeling like I was influencing and educating visitors on the history of Tuskegee University.

However, I now accept this as my new normal. Sometimes we get so caught up in the past and the things we used to have that we forget to focus on the present. I can admit that it took a long time for me to accept everything I'd lost. I'd replay over and over in my mind living in Tuskegee, walking across that stage with my degree and all the things I could've accomplished. But when my thoughts start to snowball into what could have been, I have to picture a big red stop sign to stop those thoughts.

Those types of thoughts only cause you to be miserable because you'll never know what the outcome could have been. It is very difficult to reframe your thinking. This isn't something I learned overnight; I went through years of depression before I started putting coping skills into practice. When I returned home to Chicago my father printed out a list of nephrologists (kidney doctors) that were in-network with our insurance. I was on my father's insurance as long as I was still a college student.

Having proper coverage is very important when dealing with a chronic illness. I am very blessed to have parents who were able to provide such financial support during such a major set-back in my life. I looked through the packet about the doctors, complete with which hospital each doctor practiced, their specialty, and their medical education history. A young Filipino nephrologist out of Northwestern Memorial Hospital stood out to me. I contacted the Nephrology Department at Northwestern (NMH), made an appointment and anxiously waited to meet Dr. Tauzon. When I arrived at Northwestern a week later I was impressed with how modern and well-kept the hospital was. As a patient, you notice the cleanliness first of any place you will receive care. I felt comfortable and I just knew I would receive the best care. I walked up to the Nephrology (the study of the kidneys) Department, signed in with the Receptionist, and took a seat. I didn't know what to expect. I could only hope this doctor was nice and could cure me of whatever this was. But more than anything, I was anxious to find out what exactly was going on inside of me that was causing such severe swelling. I had gained up to 20 pounds of fluid (water weight) which was very uncomfortable on my lungs, and my skin felt like it was being stretched in every direction, like a water balloon that's right at the point of bursting. I was always a petite, muscular, athletic girl, with a height of 5'1" and a healthy weight of 120. I was now about 140 and struggling to catch my breath. I also have severe asthma.

When I was younger, around the age of 10, on a hot humid day I stepped out on our back patio briefly and immediately became short of breath. I went upstairs to my room and began my Nebulizer Treatment (a machine that uses oxygen and medication to deliver relief from asthma attacks). After completing the treatment, I didn't feel any relief. I told my brother and grandfather who was watching us at the time while my parents worked. I explained to him I was short of breath and needed him to drive me to the hospital. I remember gazing out of the window in the back seat of his car gasping for air and taking my inhaler multiple times. As I think back on that situation I realize I probably oversaturated my lungs with medicine. This can cause you to block the lungs and oxygen is unable to be exchanged. I felt like my grandfather was driving two miles an hour. I was told I passed out and began foaming at the mouth. When we arrived at the Emergency Room my brother, who was 11, did the most heroic thing that I'd never live down: He carried me from the backseat of the car into the ER, shouting for help. I was intubated (a tube placed down the throat and into the lungs to assist with breathing) and kept in the hospital for over a week. I remember looking in the mirror after coming to and seeing my horrific bloodshot eyes. I've never had another episode like that due to my asthma because I began a regime of steroid inhalers that I take twice daily.

So you can imagine my discomfort with all the fluid building up. Nevertheless, I was curious to see who this doctor was that would now have my life in her hands. When my name was called, there was an average height, slim, curly haired African American Nurse with a clipboard ushering me and my father into the back. There were multiple rooms, some used for blood draws others used for exams. As I followed the nurse to the room I felt like my heart was ready to jump out of my chest. There was no turning back now, I needed to stay strong and hope for the best. She checked my vitals: height, weight, temperature, and blood pressure. This would become the routine every visit from here on out, with some visits requiring blood draws. The nurse went over and entered into the computer my health history and any medications I was currently taking. She informed me she would notify the doctor that I was ready and to wait patiently until the doctor came in. I looked around the room that was equipped with standard exam supplies, and had many posters depicting the structure of the kidneys and how they work. I was in school studying to become a nurse. I was a little familiar with the kidneys and many parts of the body. This little knowledge would go a long way as I will impress doctors with my knowledge of my condition and medical jargon.

My college courses in anatomy and physiology, microbiology, among other science courses were the foundation that motivated me to research and take an overall interest in my health condition. Some people even imply that I "overthink" things and worry too much. However, in my opinion when it comes to your health I don't think it's possible not to overthink any and every little thing. People will search the internet, obsessively looking for answers to their symptoms. You *should* always be your own advocate and do your research! I'm not saying I'm a doctor or have any medical training. But medicine isn't an exact science so a lot of treatments aren't guaranteed to work the same for everyone or even work at all. REMEMBER, there are NO GUARANTEES in medicine. I think sometimes people (myself included) put too much pressure on the *practice* of medicine and doctors to "get it right" that they forget, medical professionals are human too. I too struggle with putting all of my hope into a treatment or advice from a doctor and when the outcome isn't what you were told it would be or expected, it's natural to want to take your frustration out on them. I feel for people in the medical profession because they are verbally and sometimes physically abused by patients who are in denial about their condition, scared, frustrated, and many other feelings that chronically ill patients deal with. I'm sure there are a few doctors and nurses who wouldn't have very nice things to say about me because of my misplaced fear and anger. But as a patient it's not your intention to hurt anyone's feelings; it's just that you're so hurt, you take it out on the people closest to you. It's true: "hurt people hurt people." Which are normally loved ones, medical professionals, friends, and complete strangers. They don't understand what you're going through, so sometimes it feels like they're being careless or even insensitive to your feelings and experiences.

So, there we were in the exam room patiently/nervously waiting. Then the door opened softly and a petite Filipino, well-dressed woman with a white coat came in. She introduced herself to my father and me. She said her name was Dr. Jennifer Tauzon. She was so cute and petite, and we started a long conversation about where she shopped and where I shopped. You know girl stuff. Gaining rapport on her end, but nervous-nice on my end.

"Okay enough of the fluff. Break it down to me straight, what are we looking at here? What am I facing?" I asked.

I'm a no nonsense, no fluff kind of girl. I don't want all the sugarcoating. I need answers and solutions.

Following my demands, she said, "Well, we can't tell what is exactly going on with your kidneys without a biopsy.

However, we do know that judging by the amount of protein you're spilling into your urine it needs to be addressed right away," she said.

"What does a biopsy mean? I have an idea of what it is, but can you explain a little further what the procedure consists of and will it hurt?" I asked.

"Well, they will stick a needle in your back under local anesthesia which just numbs the area, And grab a piece of kidney tissue with the use of an ultrasound to guide them. It shouldn't hurt and they can even give you a little sedation medicine to relax you but you will be awake. Overall, it's quick and painless with a little soreness the next day," she said

"Okay, that doesn't sound too bad. But, this test will tell what this is, right?" I asked.

"Yes, once they harvest the tissue it will be looked at under a microscope to examine the tiny filters of the kidney among other structures," she said with confidence.

"Okay how soon can I have it done?" I asked.

"On your way out, the check-out desk can give you the instructions on how to make an appointment with Interventional Radiology," she said.

I was a little bummed she wasn't going to do it, but she assured me that this is what they do down there, and I'd be fine.

This would be my first procedure of many. I still have the two small dots on my back from two biopsies that will forever remind me of just how far I've come.

So we (mom, dad and I) showed up at the hospital,

registered and checked in at Interventional Radiology. The I.R. department uses radiological scans to help guide the surgeon in whichever procedure he's performing. I was then escorted to the back where I got changed into a gown, surgical cap, and footies. The nurses checked my vitals, inserted an IV and went over my medical history (which medications and any known illnesses). The doctor who would perform the biopsy came in to explain how the procedure would go and that I could take my headphones into the operating room (it definitely helped to listen to music during the procedures).

Music is my coping mechanism. It helps calm my anxiety. Many doctors were (and still are) very open to me bringing my music for procedures in which I will be awake. Or they will play Beyoncé radio for me over their speaker system. Small things like this really help the patients trust medical professionals and help ease their anxiety around the unknown of these procedures.

So, I got to the back and there was an ultrasound machine and a bunch of other machines, but the ultrasound was the only thing I recognized. I was told to lay on my stomach to expose my back. They cleaned the area with antiseptic soap. The doctor informed me there would be a small burn and a pinch like a bee sting to numb the area with Lidocaine (if I had a nickel for every time I've heard that over the last six years, I'd own the company that makes it). Lidocaine is a numbing medication just like the one you get when you go to the dentist and get that awful shot in the mouth. Well the bee sting part is the worst part of it. I've never been stung by a bee and shit, if that's how it feels, I want no part of it. It felt like a needle sticking you in your back, period. But I know the doctor saw the large tramp stamp on my lower back and thought, *oh she should be used to needles in her back* (even that poor decision was awfully painful). Either way, you *never* get used to needles in your back. So after he numbed the area, he informed me he was going to stick a larger needle in my back and I would hear some clicking sounds and feel pressure, which I did. Not long after we started, the procedure was over. He informed me he would send the kidney tissue samples off to the lab and they would have the results back for my doctor within a few days to a week.

Dr. Tauzon was always really good about getting back to me as soon as she could. When the results were in she called me to see when I could come back in with my parents to discuss the results. I was relieved that they found the cause of all the swelling I'd been having, however I was terrified because I thought the worst. What if it's cancer? What if it's Lupus? I don't know anything about kidneys or kidney diseases so of course I was going to think the worst-case scenario. But, like with anything, there's a wide range of things that could go wrong with kidneys, from not so serious to extremely serious—ranging from infections to diseases.

So we went back to Northwestern meet with Dr. Tauzon and she informed me that they found scaring in my right kidney and added that most of the time if there's something going on with one it's most likely happening to the other (not all cases, but most of the time). She informed me this scarring is caused by a disease called Focal Segmental Glomerulosclerosis. Basically the tiny filters in the kidneys become scarred and as you can imagine that can be a major issue. I never realized how much the kidneys do. They help regulate blood pressure, remove toxins from the blood, and produce urine, among so many other things. My kidneys were spilling the important proteins from my blood stream into my urine. The filters were not able to keep the proteins where they belonged. Every time I urinated I spilled five grams of protein into my urine. The average healthy person spills less than one gram. So she continued to inform me that there is no cure for this disease but there are some drugs that they believe could possibly slow the progression of it but ultimately I would go into complete renal failure, have to go on dialysis, and need a kidney transplant. Stunned, I started crying. I didn't know exactly what dialysis was but I'd heard of it before and it didn't sound like a day at the beach.

But the main takeaway is that I'd need a kidney because dialysis was just a treatment, not a cure. Then as if things couldn't get any worse she proceeded to tell me, "Oh, and if you get a new kidney, it's possible the disease could come back and attack the new kidney," with a straight look on her face.

"Wait, what?" I asked inquisitively.

So many thoughts ran through my mind as I tried to process everything she'd just told me. *What type of sick (no pun intended) s#!t is that? So I'm going to lose my kidneys, get on dialysis, get a new kidney and I could be right back in this same predicament again?? That's what you want me to comprehend ?!OK, so what the F&%K is the purpose of me going through all of this? Not saying I want to die, but how can you expect a person to live with that every day and to accept that they will never be cured of this awful disease?*

Dr. Tauzon began a regimen of immunosuppressant (exactly how it sounds, drugs that suppress your immune system) and steroids to help slow down the progression of the disease, but in my opinion it's inevitable. *It's going to progress! So what's the point? You're just buying time before starting dialysis.* Over the course of two and a half years I was put on more and more drugs: one for the swelling called a water pill that would eventually stop working as the more I peed the more it became harmful to me. The more I peed, the more protein I would lose, thus having more swelling because I would retain the fluid in my tissues. *Complete mind fuck right?* I thought urinating was supposed to help you LOSE fluids. So that took a while to understand. At times I'd try to hold my pee so I wouldn't lose the protein and swell. But, as you could imagine, that's not a very good idea. But when your body is in turmoil you don't think rationally. You'll do anything to get your old self back. At that point I hadn't fully accepted or even understood the *magnitude* of what was going on with me.

O I WAS WORKING AND GOING TO SCHOOL, trying to continue my life with this awful news looming over my head like a dark cloud and BAM! Pain hit me like a thief in the night...as though someone had broken into my house and shot me in the back while I was asleep. Although I've never been shot, I could imagine this it what it feels like. The pain was so excruciating and so sudden, I think I was more startled and confused. I glanced around the room and didn't see anyone and didn't see any blood. *So what is causing this excruciating pain*? I thought. The pain was so debilitating that I couldn't even roll over to reach my phone to call for help. My sister was asleep in the next room and I yelled her name but no response. I had to drag myself not even a few inches across my bed to reach my phone on the nightstand—and that felt like an impossible feat. I called my sister on her phone a few times before she answered and came in my room.

"What!? What?! What's wrong ?!" she called out and judging by the tears she knew we needed to call 9-1-1. I didn't know what was wrong I just knew the pain was unbearable. When the paramedics arrived they asked me, "can you walk to the stretcher?"

I explained to them, "There is no way I can even turn over." They grabbed a chair from our dining room and the three men lifted me, frozen in one position, from my bed into the chair and carried me to the ambulance. It was the middle of winter. I was only wrapped in a blanket without any shoes and even as the winter air hit my face all I could think about was the excruciating pain in my back. After they loaded me into the ambulance they began taking my vitals and asking me about my medical history. I explained to them I have a kidney disease and I'm not sure why I'm in so much pain and yes, this is the first time I've experienced any pain like this. This would be the first of many emergency rides in the back of an ambulance because of my kidney disease. While in the back of the ambulance the EMTs asked a series of questions: Are you on any medications? My past medical history, my height, weight, etc. They immediately started hooking me up to all sorts of machines and tubes. Putting electrodes on my chest to monitor my heart function. Next, they started checking my arm for a good vein (which is normally the antecubital or AC) in the crease of your elbow—that's the biggest and easiest vein to get, especially during a crisis. They immediately gave me some pain meds. But no relief. This pain in my back is still one of my top three worst pains I've ever felt. It was excruciating. We arrived at the Emergency Department where they were waiting for us with all of my information. They lifted me onto a bed because I was doubled over and crying in pain. The nurse started administering more drugs to help with the pain, taking bloodwork (blood to be analyzed by the lab) and asking more in-depth questions about my past medical history. I explained to them I had a recently diagnosed kidney disease called FSGS along with asthma and past surgeries included a nasal polypectomy. The ER doctor on call came in to speak with me; he reassured me they would do everything to keep me comfortable (which usually means strong pain meds) and run as many tests as possible to find out what was going on with me. It wasn't long before the results were in: I had a kidney infection. Apparently a urinary tract infection could travel up the ureters and into the kidneys. I would remain in the hospital for about a week, treated with multiple antibiotics and pain medicine. You can't keep an IV in for longer than four days while in the hospital. The nurse came in to change the IV, and after being stuck numerous times with no luck at getting the vein, I had had enough. As a patient I have a right to say when I have had enough, when I have reached my threshold of pain and suffering, even if it's supposed to be beneficial for my health. I would later learn that you don't have to take or do anything you don't want to do. Many aren't aware of their rights as a patient. Although the healthcare team is there to support you and do everything possible to keep you comfortable and safe, only you can be your best advocate. I've learned to ask questions about what medications I am being given, which procedures are being performed, and what the plan of care is. I can't stress enough how important it is to know what medications you're taking, how frequent, and their strength. Your healthcare providers are people too—meaning they make mistakes. There have been a few times that I was almost given the wrong medication or dose because of simple human error. Had I not been aware of these things, a simple mistake could've cost me my life. Many drugs do not interact well with each other. When you have a chronic illness you have to be careful not to mix certain drugs. It would be great to solely be able to rely on others to catch these things, but the reality of it is: your life is in your hands. You wouldn't allow a passenger to steer the car from the front seat would you? They may be able to offer their advice or observation, but ultimately you're the one driving the car when it comes to your health. I would never tell someone not to follow medical advice but understand that it is just that, *advice*. In the past, I didn't have a voice when it came to my healthcare. My mother would speak for me and interact with my doctors. I just let it be. Until, on many days I found myself alone with my healthcare team and she wasn't there to speak for me. Now many doctors and nurses are shocked when I can recite back to them all of my medications and dosages. I didn't realize how uncommon it is for patients to actually know what they're putting in their bodies every day. Many people rely on family or a medication list to remind them. However, if you can remember the many online passwords you have, you can memorize your medications. After I recovered from the kidney infection I never had another one, but I did have a couple more urinary tract infections. Having a kidney disease made me more susceptible to infections.

As you can imagine, all of this began to take a toll on me mentally and emotionally. I was struggling to manage my deteriorating health, work, and college. I was determined to complete my bachelor's degree. I wasn't going to let some kidney disease stand in the way of completing my educational goals. I'd had it all planned out since high school. I took night classes at the community college, dually enrolled with my regular high school courses. I took a science course and lab that would remain beneficial years later. I knew at a young age I wanted to work in healthcare or science. I remember in elementary school I asked for a microscope for Christmas and I'd sit in my room for hours projecting the bug-smashed slides on to my bedroom wall in the dark (nerdy, I know). Then, in high school I excelled in microbiology and industrialized chemistry classes. It was then my biology teacher. Mrs. Barker, who sat me down and told me, "You are a nerd and don't you ever forget that or let anyone tell you different because those are the successful people in this world."

She encouraged me to pursue honors microbiology, which I got an A in, might I add. At that time I knew I found my niche. This foundation in science would later go on to help me understand how bacteria and viruses work at the cellular level. This helped me understand whenever I was ill and the doctors would prescribe certain medications. For example, I understand the process of narrowing down a specific strain of bacteria. If the doctors suspect you have a bacterial infection, they typically start with a broad spectrum antibiotic (which means it will kill a broad range of bacteria until they can narrow it down after further tests to a specific strain). I wouldn't know this had I not excelled in those science courses. It was decided: I was going to be a Certified Registered Nurse Anesthetist. This would require at least four years to complete a Bachelor of Science in Nursing and additional emergency room experience, and then completing a program in anesthesia. I had my whole life mapped out. I would complete all of the school necessary, then go on to form a partnership with an anesthesiologist and another nurse. In my free time I began researching Ads that were looking for CRNAs to join their partnership, even traveling across the country. But what interested me in the partnership is that you split the money three ways as opposed to being contracted to a hospital. When I want something, I make it happen and research it to no end to the point of obsession. It consumes me. I wanted this more than anything. By the time I enrolled full-time in College I was looking so far ahead into my future that I knew nothing would stand in my way of achieving my goals. What attracted me to the anesthesia profession is how drugs work on the nervous system. Technically, you're still in pain, but the drugs work on the receptors that transmit pain to stop the pain signals from going to your brain. How can you not be fascinated by that? Medicine is amazing and has come so far, and fortunately I would experience, time after time, the wonders of this practice. I've had more surgeries than I could count and each time the anesthesiologist came back to talk to me, I'd pick his or her brain. They'd let me look at the computer of all of my vitals and notes. I'd tell them of how I dreamed of having their job and not be on the other end. They all tried to encourage me that I shouldn't give up on my dream and that I could still make it happen. Many times, as I was being put under anesthesia, I'd get really talkative and ask about the drugs. I'd ask if they were giving me the "Michael Jackson Drug" Propofol. That would get a good laugh out of everyone in the operating room, but they knew what was coming next. It was a thick white milky color and burned like hell! But, by the time it burns your arm off going into your IV, within seconds you're off to sleep. That pain is one you will never forget. I dread it every time I have to have surgery. They tell you, *we mixed it with lidocaine to decrease the burning.* But, I'd hate to know what it feels like without the lidocaine. So how could Michael Jackson have been getting IV Propofol every night among other drugs? Man, I couldn't imagine. But I digress.

There Are No Mistakes Only Lessons

AT THIS POINT, I WAS OVERWHELMED. I didn't have the words to label the feelings as overwhelmed, I just knew I was sick and tired of being sick and tired. I felt like I was drowning and nobody around me understood. Physically, I was overloaded with fluids. Mentally, I was drowning in thoughts over depression and struggling to cope. Spiritually I was struggling to stay hopeful as I had only been sick for a couple of years, but knowing that I would still end up on dialysis and need a kidney transplant was overwhelming to live with every day …just knowing what was potentially ahead of me and how sick I was at the time. Emotionally, I was drained, and that's when I decided this wasn't going to be a life I wanted to live. I was definitely drowning in every aspect of my life. I felt like nobody around me even cared. It was like they wanted me to just keep pushing without even acknowledging what I was going through. I truly believe they were in denial. I was, too, because I forced myself to carry on all of this weight until I broke. One day I was threatened with being evicted because I was short on my rent. My hours at work were cut because I was in and out of the hospital so much I wasn't a very reliable worker. Yet still, my job would allow me to come back to work, but I wasn't making much money. So falling short on my rent was the straw that broke the camel's back. I fell into a hole I felt I couldn't get out of. I remember sending a text to my family and friends letting them know I loved them and I couldn't do it anymore. I looked through all the pills I had and found the only pain killers. I opened the bottle and estimated about 40 pills. I just knew that would do the trick. I took them all and prepared to leave this world. My brother was home and I assume after receiving the text message he came and found me in the kitchen. He called 9-1-1. When the paramedics came, they were asking all sorts of questions,

"Ma'am, what did you take? It's important you tell us so we can help you", one paramedic asked.

"I don't want help; I want to die." I responded in a drowsy voice.

My brother gave them the bottle and they loaded me in the back of the ambulance. When I arrived at the nearby hospital they immediately started hooking me up to monitors, checking my blood pressure, heart rate, temperature and inserting IVs. They gave me the highest dose of IV Benadryl (I guess to counteract the drugs I'd already taken) I'd ever had, and I felt it pulling me down into this deep sleep. It's weird—because I was terrified. I had prepared to die just some few minutes earlier, but at that moment I knew I had made a mistake. Luckily the pills I took weren't strong enough to kill me, but could've done significant damage to my liver. Thankfully they hadn't. So from there I spent the night and got transferred by ambulance to a psychiatric floor at a major hospital. I spent a week there because the floor is only acute-care, meaning you get intensive psychotherapy, and most patients are released within a week. When I first arrived, it was in the middle of the night, about 3 a.m., after spending hours in the ER at the previous hospital, I was exhausted and annoyed. They took all of my personal belongings, including anything with strings (for obvious reasons). The only thing I had was a blanket and a gown. They took me into a small room on a quiet floor, similar to a normal hospital floor with rooms, but this floor had a double security door, pay phones, and a small kitchenette/eating area. In other words, you had everything you'd need on this floor because you weren't going anywhere until a doctor signed off on your release. So I was in this office room with a nurse who began taking my vitals and going through the intake process. It took over an hour, with me signing dozens of papers and receiving the rules of the floor. The nurse gave me the usual script on how things would go. I would get up for breakfast then attend what they called "groups" throughout the day. Mealtime actually became a source of comradery for us. We'd all sit together and barter for different food items and everyone always laughed at me, because I was so tiny but scribbled "2x" of every item on my menu sheet. The first group I attended each morning started with each patient introducing themselves (since there were always people being admitted and being released to go home). So after we introduced ourselves, the group leader (which was typically a psychiatric nurse) would let us know what the schedule would consist of for the day. He would ask us to go around and discuss our goals and what we'd like to accomplish for the day. Some would include working on anxiety or staying focused. We typically attended five groups a day. Each group had a different focus or objective. We would attend one-on-one sessions with the therapists, and creative groups where we would paint or make different things. I would definitely say being on that psych floor changed my life. There, I received the validation I needed that I never realized I was missing: someone to simply say, "It's OK to be angry or upset about your condition." As simple as it may sound, the moment I was no longer forced to put on a facade like I had it all together, I felt a huge weight lifted off of me. When I shared my story with the nurses and other patients, I felt the compassion I was always missing.

Sometimes our families are struggling to cope just like we are. They don't always have the right things to say. They want you to fight and just get through it, but they don't understand the amount of pressure that puts on the patient whose body is in turmoil and a lot of other things they don't have control over. You're telling that person, *you'll get through it,* but not giving them any direction *how*—and it is kind of like false hope, because you *don't* know if they'll get through it or not. But, I understand the family not understanding how to provide encouragement. I truly feel all patients and their families should attend family counseling on how to cope with chronic illness, just like someone with an addiction goes to rehab: usually their family would attend some sort of counseling to stop the enabling. Many patients and families are in denial of the condition and just how severe it is so I believe that contributes to the pressure they add to *be well.*

The patient just wants their old self back and it's hard to accept that this is your life now. I had a very difficult time accepting this as my "new normal" so how could I expect my family to accept it? Especially when I was forcing myself to do all the things I used to do. That gave me a false sense of reality, thus making my family not really see just how bad things were with me. However, no matter how much you try to explain to your family what's going on, they will only see what they want. They can only come to terms with it in their own time, if they do at all. Somehow you have to be OK if they don't. I spent many years struggling with getting people around me to understand what I was going through, until I realized that it's OK if they don't get it. They never will. Because they aren't in my shoes and I would never wish this upon anyone. So...I'm grateful they really don't understand the magnitude of it—because if they did, I truly don't think they could handle it any better than they're handling what they barely understand now. I tell my family they only see about 80 percent of what I truly go through, but we all have things we experience that we'd never tell a soul, like those moments when you're all alone and begging God to put you out of your misery. Your family doesn't see those moments. Plus, as a patient you're experiencing it in every way possible spiritually, emotionally, mentally, and physically. They're only watching you from the outside; I do understand that it hurts them emotionally to watch you go through it, but I think many families want you to care about how *they feel about* your situation. I had to realize it wasn't up to me to validate their feelings. I was in the fight of my life. How could I expend any of my energy worrying about how they feel when I was struggling to deal with my own feelings and *physically* fight? I learned through a lot of therapy that no matter how much I tried to gain their approval, it was an impossible feat. I was just wasting my energy trying to prove myself to people who probably didn't even live up to their own expectations. Once I started learning to reserve this much-needed energy for myself, I started to feel better mentally, emotionally, spiritually, and physically. I'm not saying I don't still battle with depression. However, it isn't because I'm succumbing to the pressures of my family.

I started to have the energy to focus on my health and the daily work it takes to live every day. I started noticing my body was healing faster, my bloodwork improved, and I felt motivated to fight. So once I was discharged from the psych floor, I was armed with the tools I needed to cope. They taught us coping skills, such as doing things we enjoy when we start to feel depressed or overwhelmed, and to reach out to someone, whether it be family, friends, or healthcare providers. The worst thing I did was keep everything bottled up inside until I couldn't take it anymore and tried to end my life. So now when I'm feeling depressed I make sure to talk about it with a few people, my therapist included. But if I still don't feel any better, I know I can always check myself into a psychiatric floor and they will give me a safe supportive environment to properly deal with my depression. It took a lot of "work" on myself mentally and emotionally to humble myself and be introspective enough to acknowledge when I'm sliding down that slippery slope of depression. Then, to not only acknowledge it, but to put my pride aside and figure out what my step to receive help will be, whether it's checking myself in or talking to my doctor about how I'm feeling. Because one of the main things I've learned is that everyone deals with depression. I think the big misconception is that you are "crazy" or have a mental disorder in order to be affected by depression. I've learned that all it takes is to go through something traumatic in life and next thing you know, you find yourself alone rocking back and forth in a corner ready to end it all. For most of us, we weren't taught coping skills at an early age so when life happens we typically don't know how to deal with the curve balls life throws at us. I think like most 20-somethings I looked at life through rose colored glasses. We think, *graduate from high school then go on to college, get a good job after graduation and settle down.* That's what most of us think life is supposed to be like. But for many people I know, life doesn't go as planned.

W HEN I HAD MY NERVOUS BREAKDOWN, I wasn't even in renal failure yet. I was basically waiting to get worse. You see, you have to meet certain criteria to be considered in renal failure and then placed on dialysis, as if it's some magical treatment that will cure you of this awful disease. Chronic kidney disease has five stages. In the first stage, your kidneys are still functioning normally so urine tests or genetic tests usually point to kidney disease so this just requires observation. The second stage is similar to the first, in that you only have a mild decrease in kidney function and still are just being observed. The third stage is moderately reduced kidney function with continued observation. Now stage four is where the fun stuff begins. This is the stage you're planning for renal failure and start talking about treatment options such as transplantation or dialysis. Stage five is complete loss of renal function also known as end-stage renal disease. I remember being in stage four but not quite in complete renal failure. However, the symptoms are so bad, you want the doctors to put you out of your misery (not saying I wanted to be on dialysis either). So at this point, you're eligible to be considered for a transplant program. The program has to review your chart and verify that you also meet certain criteria similar to starting dialysis. You have to be so bad that there's no hope for your current organs and they feel it's necessary to give you a new organ. I mean can you imagine how bad off you have to be at this point? I felt like I was drowning in my own fluids. By this point I was swelling so bad that I couldn't retain any protein in my blood. (You need proteins in your blood to evenly disperse your fluids, otherwise any fluid in your body will spread to your tissues.) So every time I urinated I would lose so much protein (17 grams—and normal is less than 1 gram in your urine) that it would make me swell even more. I remember having my usual blood work done and the laboratory called to check and see if this was a mistake or if I was a real person because the albumin (protein) level was so low in my blood that they couldn't calculate it. I was then referred to the transplant center at the hospital (Northwestern Memorial Hospital) where I was already receiving care. You can go to any hospital's transplant program in your region, as long as you're able to get there for pre-transplant testing and follow-up care. I made an initial appointment to go in and learn what kidney transplant is all about. They advised me to contact anyone who was open to donate their kidney to me and invite them to come listen to the lecture given by the transplant team which included nurses, surgeons and case workers. At this point, I hadn't started dialysis yet and knew nothing about the transplant process. The goal is to have a donor before starting dialysis or to be on dialysis as little as possible. More than 10 family members went down with me to the transplant meeting. It was an overwhelming show of love and support, even if most of them couldn't donate. Just the mere fact that they went down there meant a lot to me. Sometimes, we get so caught up in the disappointment by people who don't show up for things, that we don't acknowledge the ones who are actually there. Like this one time I went to a friend's birthday dinner and the entire time she complained about all the people who cancelled, instead of honoring the people who were there. It made us feel as though our time and presence wasn't good enough. Always remember to celebrate the ones who show up for things even if you expect them to be there anyway. No one's time or support is owed to you.

At the end of the informational meeting they all went down to the laboratory to get their blood drawn to see if any of them were a match to donate to me. I was in the exam room being interviewed by nephrologists, transplant nurses, transplant surgeons, social workers, and pharmacists that discussed with me what to expect before and after transplantation. They also wanted to ensure I was mentally and physically prepared to accept a transplant. (You'll understand later on why this is so important.) Next, the nephrologist completed a history and physical exam. Then the social worker spoke with me about depression and my previous suicide attempt. She asked me if I still felt suicidal. And of course I told her *no* because at this point I was under the care of a psychiatrist for depression, but I also acknowledged that at this point depression was something I would always deal with and learn to manage throughout my life as long as I have a chronic illness. The transplant meeting was in February 2011, and my condition continued to worsen. While I waited to be evaluated by the transplant team, which means after meeting you, they go into a meeting where they discuss everyone's cases and decide if you're worse off yet, but healthy enough to be considered for a transplant (crazy, I know), my condition continued to worsen and I couldn't wait any longer. Plus, I was told that once they decided on a donor (after reviewing their health questionnaires and blood results) it could take up to three months for that donor to be completely tested before a transplant surgery could take place.

So I needed to make some very important decisions regarding my health. I was going to be placed on dialysis until further notice. Dialysis is a process in which a machine cleans your blood *for* you, also known as an artificial kidney machine. It takes the place of your kidneys when yours are no longer functioning properly. There are two types of dialysis: peritoneal dialysis and hemodialysis. Peritoneal dialysis works by using the peritoneum (a lining of the abdominal cavity) membrane to attract water (osmosis) and toxins (diffusion) into the abdominal cavity that you fill with a sugar based solution (dextrose). Each solution has a certain concentration that will either "pull" a little or a lot of fluids. Each instillation of this solution, letting it "dwell," then draining it is called a cycle. Each person has a prescribed number of cycles that their doctor calculates using a formula that will give you an adequate amount of dialysis (cleaning your blood). For example, my treatment consisted of six cycles over a period of 10 hours. I then had an extra dwell time of three hours (called a midday exchange). So my overall treatment time is 13 hours with seven exchanges. Some people will have a midday exchange if they need extra dialysis for different reasons. The second type of dialysis treatment is called hemodialysis. Hemo refers to blood, that's the best way to differentiate between the two. During hemodialysis all of your blood, which is about 1.5 gallons, is drained by way of a permanent vascular access in your arm. This vascular access, which a surgeon creates where he merges your veins to create a super vein, which is something you will have for the rest of your life once it is in place. Whether you use it or not, once the veins are merged they can't be un-merged... well, there really is no point in unmerging them. Any who, at every treatment a trained healthcare professional will gain access to this super vein by sticking two needles into it. Each needle is attached to two tubes (a blue and a red) one pulls the blood from your body and sends it to a machine that will run it through a filter that cleans it and removes your fluids then it is returned back into the body through the opposite color tube. There is also another type of access called a subclavian catheter, which is placed into the heart through a different surgical process. This type of catheter isn't recommended for permanent use. It carries a higher risk of infection. Since it is placed into your heart and comes out through the skin, bacteria can get into your bloodstream and your heart; those are the hardest infections to treat. I've heard an infection like that can be life-threatening and land you in the hospital for months, if you survive. Lucky for me, I had a subclavian catheter for years and never got an infection. When I was told it was time for me to start dialysis I wanted to do more research before I got the permanent access in my arm. So I opted for a chest catheter. I walked around with a catheter hanging out of my chest for many years. It made it difficult for me to wear certain clothes and to shower (I wasn't supposed to shower at all). But I don't understand how you can tell a grown woman with lady parts to not shower? I understood that if I would've gotten any moisture or water into the chest catheter that I could've gotten an infection. But me being hard-headed, I took my chances. I'd tape up the chest catheter with a waterproof bandage, gauze, plastic, and medical tape. I did this routine every day and angled myself away from the water as not to get the plastic wet. I tried to take extra precaution because I wasn't even supposed to be showering. But things like this are just some of the ways I adapted to being on dialysis as a young woman. These were things I had to do for myself in order to keep some of my normalcy and sanity. For me, it was very important that

I found certain clothes that hid my chest catheter or I would find a one-shoulder shirt (they came back in style when I was on dialysis) and I'd wear it backwards if it didn't cover the side my catheter was on. I've had three catheters placed on my left side and two on my right side. They had to alternate sides because of scar tissue that develops in the artery every time you have one placed. Initially, I started out on hemodialysis because I didn't learn much about peritoneal dialysis and the last thing on your mind is doing it at home by yourself. I remember my first week of dialysis like it was yesterday. As cliché as it sounds, all the other days run together like a movie, but the first week I don't think I'll ever forget.

I'd just gotten the chest catheter placed a few days before so it was still very sore, but it could be used right away. My aunt Tracie, who at the time had been diagnosed with pancreatic cancer (God rest her soul), came with me to the "center." It was filled with old people in wheel chairs and had canes. I was the youngest person there. You could see the shock on their faces when I came in and checked in as a patient. I will always get the *"you're too young to be on dialysis look"* as long as I'm a renal patient. Dialysis is thought to be an older person's treatment like 70 and older but I am here to tell you kidney disease doesn't discriminate. I am seeing more and more young people on dialysis. And by young I mean 20s and 30s. I am not exactly sure what is causing this rise of kidney disease in younger people. My theory is unfortunately all the chemicals we put in our foods and bodies now that many years ago did not exist. And now we're seeing the effects of those chemicals. So anywho, I checked in and the receptionist told me to have a seat and that a nurse would come to get me when it was my turn to go back. So, just as she said, a nurse came to get me from the waiting room and led me to another huge open room with about 25 chairs all lined against the wall in a horseshoe shape. Each chair had its own hemodialysis machine and a TV monitor that consisted of the internet, cable, and radio stations for your entertainment pleasure. This is important for patients because most treatments run about four hours and if yours is any less, then you're lucky. I saw many patients already "hooked up" to their machines with their blood circulating through them. I was terrified. I remember the especially sweet nurse named Ozzie (I'm not sure if that was her real name) introduced herself, and could tell I was extremely frightened. She attempted to reassure me that everything would be OK. I remember asking her if the treatment would hurt and if I would feel anything. She reassured me that I wouldn't, but I don't care how many times someone tells you that having all of your blood drained out and put back in won't hurt—your brain can't process that. As she sat me down and explained the procedure of removing my bandages that covered my chest catheter, I began to cry. I cried the entire four hours of my treatment and every day after for the first week. My aunt came with me a few times and held my hand as three times a week we started the process all over again. Even though she was fighting her own battle with pancreatic cancer, she was able to accompany me and comfort me because we shared the same struggle of the unknown around our health. I was inconsolable many days. I think the reality sunk in that there was no going back. In order to live, I had a date three times a week with this center, these nurses, and this machine. As the days passed, different family members came with me. Many days my mom came toward the last couple hours of my treatment after she got off work. We'd play board games and she'd take me home happy to be out of that place. I'm sure being hooked up to a machine is the last thing anyone wants to watch their loved one go through. But actually being *the one* hooked up to the machine and having to put your life in someone else's hands is something I wouldn't wish on my worst enemy.

Six months after starting hemodialysis I was informed that my kidneys were still producing urine. Now, remember I told you that my kidneys were spilling all of my protein? So that's what was causing the swelling right? But the dialysis machine took over the work for my kidneys and was effectively removing my toxins and fluids, so while the swelling seemed to go down I was still losing my protein. It was hard to understand that the dialysis was helping me, but my own kidneys were harming me by fighting to still work. My transplant team suggested that I have my native kidneys removed. Most people with renal failure don't have their native kidneys removed because typically the kidneys will stop working and shrivel up like prunes. Well as you'll come to see I'm not like *most* people. There's always something crazy happening with this body of mine. I feel like I'm in a body with a mind of its own. It's hard to accept sometimes that no matter how hard you try or what efforts you put in, that you don't have any control. So who better to remove my kidneys than the transplant team, considering that they harvest many kidneys when they do living donor transplants? They informed me that I had two options, I could let them inject some sort of poison into my kidneys to get them to shut down or I could undergo a laparoscopic (using a small incision to insert a scope) procedure to have them surgically removed. Um, I opted for the latter, for obvious reasons. Injecting me with poison didn't sound too safe. You see, people will only do to you what you allow, and that transcends many areas of life. I trusted the doctors, but if they were even considering injecting me with poison, I think it was best to trust my own intuition on this one and opt for the surgical removal. I also trusted that the surgeons have mastered the procedure of removing kidneys. Now they do it laparoscopically to avoid making a huge incision to go in and cut the kidneys and then needing another large incision to pull them out through. I only have two three-inch scars on each side of my abdomen and one down the middle where they were removed (instead of three long six-inch-or-more scars across my abdomen). Nowadays, more surgeons are opting to do more procedures laparoscopically because they're less invasive. Laparoscopic procedures cut down on the infection risk and damage to surrounding tissue. It's easier to create a small incision and slide a scope in so the surgeons can view what the camera sees on a monitor before cutting. This also allows them to see things that they may not be able to see or would have to reach their hands in to move certain organs around. The less anyone has to reach their hands into you, the better for you and them. One of the top hospitals in Chicago is now doing robotic kidney transplants. A surgeon operates the robot from another room. This prevents the risk of human error and lessens the risk of infection. A robot can precisely make an incision based on measurements inputted into a computer. I would trust the robot to do my kidney transplant. At this point, computers have become an important part of our lives. Unfortunately, I'm sure this puts a lot of humans out of work, but, in surgery, I'm sure there will always be doctors and nurses overseeing the robots. They removed my native kidneys and the surgery wasn't as bad as I thought. I didn't even have stitches or staples. Nowadays they put surgical glue over the incisions or surgical tape and after a couple of weeks it falls off when the skin underneath has healed. I still was bed-ridden and couldn't really move too much for about a week.

Unfortunately, I developed pneumonia because I laid in bed all day. This is common after surgery if you don't move around during the majority of your recovery—which isn't hard to do when you're in so much pain. Pneumonia is a bacterial infection in the lungs that causes mucous build up and can be characterized by a nasty cough and rattling sound when the patient breathes. I was re-admitted into the hospital and given IV antibiotics to kill the bacteria in my lungs. I've had pneumonia quite a few times over my lifespan. You often hear of people with weakened immune systems that die of not the disease like cancer or AIDS but of pneumonia because you need a pretty strong immune system along with the antibiotics to fight it off. I was blessed to have overcome pneumonia well over five times in my short 20-something years of life.

I can say it was very weird for me emotionally, to have my native kidneys removed. I felt like *once you have organs you were born with removed there is no turning back...there is no hope of them ever being cured of this awful disease.* If there were a magical cure developed that day, without kidneys, I wouldn't even be able to receive it. I felt a part of me missing. I even felt lighter in weight. It's like they took a small part of my soul out with them. At that point, reality set in again just how dialysis-dependent I'd become and would remain until I received a kidney transplant. Even though my kidneys were causing me more harm than good, just producing urine let me know they were in there and still fighting to work. After the surgery, the urine stopped altogether. I asked the surgeon for the picture of my kidneys (I still have it today). They looked nothing like you see on illustrations. They weren't a reddish brown color. They were in a blue surgical dish, bloody, and the left was far more swollen than the right. They were about the size of my fists and look like oval shaped muscles. I wondered, *how do I even know if these are mine? What if this is some standard picture they send to all of their patients? What are they going to do with them? Just throw them in the trash? Use them for research?* I'm not exactly sure what happened to my little kidney babies, but when the urine stopped, I knew they were gone indefinitely. I returned to hemodialysis three times a week at the center hooked up to an artificial kidney machine. You get two choices: dialysis or death. Pick one. The latter doesn't seem like much of a choice but for some. It IS a choice. Many of us struggle with needing to have control and I don't just mean chronically ill people: healthy people included. With kidney disease you relinquish that control to the machine and your body. Many people choose suicide because it gives them something to have control over: death. Since none of us knows when our time to go will be, living with that uncertainty can be very scary and anxiety provoking. For some people, being on dialysis isn't how they want to live their lives. They feel that they used to be active, and to have to be hooked up to machine for three days a week isn't who they're used to being. So they opt to not go to their treatments—I've heard of at least two people who've done this. They committed suicide that way, because without three to four days of dialysis you'll die from all the toxin build up and fluid overload. I can completely understand the patient's point of view because when I first started out, I was in shock. I was terrified and really couldn't understand how I went from an active college student to a dialysis patient. I had my whole life planned out and this felt like a nightmare I couldn't shake. I can't stress enough how much I wanted to just wake up and feel relieved that it wasn't reality and that it was, in fact, a nightmare. But no, that never happened. I woke up every day to the same reoccurring nightmare. You mourn the loss of your old self. You think about all the things you'd done before this shit happened to you. Then to watch all of your peers around you move on with their lives, get married, have kids, advance in their careers—it was very difficult for me. You think, *what if this never happened to me? Would I too be enjoying all of the great things life has to offer?* But I've learned that doing that (mulling over the what ifs) isn't very helpful because the thing about life is: you can't go back and change any of it. You have to play the hand you were dealt. Plus, I try to put things into perspective. I truly believe that even though I have a kidney disease, I'm blessed to not have cancer or a very terminal illness. With dialysis, a kidney patient can still live a life, it may not be the life they want to live, but it's still a life. I had a difficult time the first couple of years adjusting to dialysis. It felt like with every treatment there were complications. My blood pressure would go up really high and the healthcare team feared I would stroke-out during the treatment. Then, by the end, it would drop really low, and as soon as I'd stand up I'd feel very faint, sometimes even feeling like I was going to black-out. Many days I'd arrive to my treatment by a medicar service and leave in an ambulance. On this one particular day I had a seizure while hooked up to the machine. I was told the patient next to me noticed and alerted the nurses. I don't remember much; I faintly remember the paramedics asking me questions. Then I was told I had another seizure in the emergency room. None of this I remember. I was given anti-seizure meds during a weeklong stay. I was told I didn't need any long term meds because it was a dialysis-related seizure. I'd go on to have two dialysis-related seizures that could've been potentially fatal, but I was blessed that each time someone was home or nearby to help. Another time after dialysis, I got home and wasn't feeling too well, which is pretty normal afterward. I started to feel faint. So I sat down on the couch to try to compose myself (usually sitting down helps to bring your blood pressure up because standing and laying down makes it lower), but that didn't seem to help; I knew then I needed to go to the hospital. I asked my mom to take me; about a block away things started to get darker, like it was turning night very fast, but it was still the afternoon. I noticed it began with my peripheral. By the time we arrived at the ER, I couldn't see a thing. I could hear everyone, but everything was pitch black. I was certain I had my eyes wide open. The nurses were waving their hands in front of my face asking me if I could see them and what color shirts they had on and how many fingers they were holding up. I was hysterical by this point because all I could think was that I'd be blind forever. I saw nothing. Pitch black. Darkness. This was definitely one of the most terrifying experiences while on dialysis. There were plenty, but this is in my top three. I received some medicine and woke up the next day with my vision restored. I was told because of very high blood pressure the blood flow to the occipital (eyes) nerves was restricted and caused temporary blindness. The following days were spent in the hospital making sure my blood pressure was under control before I could go home. I experienced double vision and blood in the back of my eyes. I saw yellow and red streaks on the wall. Sometimes my mind would play terrible tricks on me: I thought I was seeing outlines of rabbits and spiders. And the same when I closed my eyes. As you can imagine, many sleepless nights ensued. This went on for a couple of weeks. I even needed a pair of glasses to help with my vision. I have always had 20/20 vision—on the bright side, I looked cute in my glasses. Thankfully, my vision completely improved after about a year. I would experience this phenomenon (blindness) one more time while on dialysis. When your body is in turmoil and isn't used to the treatment no matter what you do (taking medicine regularly and eating better) it will still do some very unpredictable things.

WHILE ON DIALYSIS YOU DO A LOT OF SOUL-SEARCHING, partially because you spend a lot of time alone while hooked up to a machine. It's in times of quiet and stillness that all of the things you hate about yourself come up. Being busy is easy; most people wouldn't agree with this statement, but just hear me out. When you're constantly on the go you don't really have time to get to the root of your issues; you just bury them and keep pushing forward. After all, that's what many of us were taught to do. I guess it's a survival tool; because you have to suppress your emotions in order to appear strong and continue fighting daily battles. Being on dialysis forces you to slow down. Many people have treatments ranging from four hours to 13 hours, depending on the modality. For many, in the beginning, until you become acclimated with the treatment and the mere thought that this is now your life, everything is forced on hold: school, work, even family. You will need an access established for your treatment, which requires surgery. Dialysis comes first, because, after all, it's your lifeline. You learn a lot about yourself when you have ample time to think and dissect every part of your life, past, present and what you hope the future will hold. But I've learned that the past can't be changed and the future hasn't come yet. So if you spend most of your time in either place you aren't living in the present. It wasn't until I started dialysis that I really started living in the present. Being on dialysis you never know what's going to arise physically. I learned how to "check-in" with myself daily; making mental notes of my overall health. Asking myself, *"Do you feel faint? Do you think your blood pressure is high or low? Do you feel any numbness or tingling in your extremities?* (That meant my potassium was high.) *Does your heart feel like it's racing? Does your skin feel itchy? Are you feeling dehydrated?"*

Therapy has taught me how to "check-in" with my emotions to assess how I'm feeling so I am always aware if my depression is lurking around the corner or if I need to simply address any feelings. I am learning to break the unhealthy habit of suppressing my emotions. I took this concept and applied it to my physical wellbeing. It has proven to be very effective. This has prevented me from going through a lot of physical and emotional crises. I can feel the warning signs when something isn't right within my body. I can then seek help or properly address the situation; it can be as simple as checking my blood pressure and taking meds if necessary. Many times I've gone to the emergency room and told the staff what was wrong with me before even being evaluated. I am very in tune with my body. The healthcare team will ask you, "Does this feel like anything that's happened to you before?" I appreciate the healthcare teams that really listen to the patients and understand that nobody knows a patient better than her/himself. They are only seeing a glimpse of your life. Blood work/tests are only a snapshot of your illness. Only you will ever know your complete history because you've lived it. I have much respect for healthcare teams who do their best to figure out what's wrong with someone after only seeing them for a few hours in an emergency situation.

SINCE I'M IN THERAPY REGULARLY with an amazing therapist, we do a lot of spiritual work along with emotional and mental healing. I truly believe your mental, emotional, physical, and spiritual wellbeing are all interconnected. When one is in bad shape, it is very hard to achieve equilibrium between all of them. For example, by my physical wellbeing being in shambles, it in turn influences me to have negative thoughts (mental), it made me question my purpose and connection with God (spiritual), and also have unstable moods (emotional). Whenever something comes up with my illness it is so easy to go into a negative mental state. For some reason, it is always easier to accept negative thoughts over positive ones. It takes a lot of practice to reshape those negative thoughts into positive ones, especially when the situation may be overwhelmingly grim. You start to think about all the possible negative outcomes. Your thoughts begin to snowball and before you know it, you've dug yourself into this hole of depression. That's when the stop sign skill really comes in handy. Sometimes I say, *"STOP, hammer time!"* accompanied by the hammer dance, just to make myself lighten up and get out of my head. Your head can be a very dark place if you let it. I've made a conscious decision that I will not be a prisoner of my own thoughts. You have thousands of thoughts a day, probably millions. So why give weight to the negative ones, when you can just as easily give that weight to the positive ones? Sometimes we give unrealistic validation to the negative ones, and they really don't have any validity behind them. The brain is programmed to have many thoughts throughout the day that come and go. You can let the negative ones be as fleeting as all the other unimportant thoughts you have. But instead, we let them stick around and hang out, mull them over a million times, and carry them with us throughout the day even weeks, talking about it over and over again with different people. Many people don't even want to hear it, but we get so infatuated with one negative thought that in consumes us. I truly believe your thoughts are a conversation with the universe. So I try to be mindful about what I am thinking and saying because thoughts become words, then words become actions. I haven't quite mastered this skill but I think just becoming aware of it is enough to help you change the way you think. Of all the work I've done on myself, I'd definitely have to say I still struggle with this one. I will be a renal patient as long as I live, which means I will always struggle with fear and anxiety around my health. A friend of mine once told me anxiety is excitement's ugly cousin. So if I can only remember that all of my anxiety can be reshaped into excitement with just one thought, I can drastically improve the amount of weight I give to the negative thoughts. I find it helpful to remember all of the blessings and wonderful things in my life when I start to worry about the negative. I think about how grateful I am to still be alive, to have my family, to have overcome so many obstacles. I'm learning to live in the moment each day. I tell people that the present will one day become just a memory. Why not make the best of it now even when things aren't going the best?

Give it up (to God, that is)…

WHEN I WAS FIRST DIAGNOSED I was told I'd need a kidney transplant to live a dialysis-free life again. I didn't know that before receiving a transplant, God would put me through so many trials and tests. Many times I thought someone would just gladly hand me their kidney, no strings attached, and the testing process would be a breeze. Well, as we know, nothing in life that's worth having will be easy to obtain. God needs to know that we're ready for the blessing He will bestow upon us. You have to be *tried and true*, as I call it. If He can't trust you to manage dialysis and everything that comes with it, how can He trust you to receive and care for a whole organ? I truly believe you have to struggle first before you can truly appreciate the magnitude of receiving an organ. Sure, it may seem unfair that many people don't have to fight for an organ. However, I believe everyone has a fight of their own. I've learned not to look over into someone else's yard and assume just because their fight isn't the same as mine that they don't have one. We all have a purpose, and finding out what that purpose is, I believe, is our life's work. The road to that purpose may not be an easy straight forward one, in fact it usually is like a winding twisting road with many detours and roadblocks. In our minds we have a map all laid out of how we think life should go. I am learning to forgo the map and put all of my trust in God's plan for my life. But the question is how do you know you are living up to His standards for your life? How do you know you are following His map and not your own?

As I neared my four-year mark on the transplant list and still doing home dialysis every night, something shifted in me.

I became more and more aware of how selfish I needed to be in order to survive.

I gave away so much of my energy to people who didn't reciprocate the same amount of energy to me because they are energy leeches. I learned to stop giving away my precious energy—that I needed for myself to continue to fight— to others.

I can admit I gave away my energy to useless things and activities. I'd often just go for drives around the area or go to restaurants alone. Because, at one point, that brought me great satisfaction. I could've spent that time doing far more productive things, but I was a prisoner of my own situation. Believing it was OK to waste time doing meaningless things, because I didn't feel meaningful. There are so many lies we tell ourselves about ourselves. I had to redefine what *having meaning* is. In our society if you don't have a degree or career to prove you are worthy then it's very easy to feel isolated. I often felt like the world was passing me by while I was stuck on dialysis. You definitely lose a lot of your youth. You deal with things and accept death every day, in case it comes for you. Most 20-somethings don't live that kind of torture every day; they're busy thinking about growing older and advancing in their careers.

I'd always been interested in helping others and volunteering with many organizations. In college I'd mentor children of incarcerated parents; we'd hang out with them or take them roller-skating to give them a sense of belonging and support. This always fulfilled me. I truly enjoy making a difference in someone's life and hopefully improving their life in any way I can. I give my time and energy from the heart because I believe it is my life's work to be of service to others. I have always had more than enough growing up so I often feel so "filled up" that I give of myself to others, but instead of it depleting me I feel even more fulfilled. This is how I know that philanthropy is my purpose and calling on my life. I also volunteered during President (then Senator) Barack Obama's campaign for Presidency at his first Caucus in Iowa, 2007. After being diagnosed, I reached out to my aunt (through marriage) who, by coincidence, has the same disease (FSGS), overcame being on dialysis, and then received a kidney transplant from her son's best friend. She told me about the National Kidney Foundation of Illinois. She's very involved, and suggested I go to their website and also get involved. This was exactly what I was looking for. There were so many resources, from newsletters, to patient testimonials, and ample volunteer opportunities. I volunteered on a few campaigns such as a partnership with Gift of Hope and Donate Life of Illinois to raise awareness about donation. We were trained at the Gift of Hope facility on how to debunk myths and provide people with correct information in the Driver Services Facilities, to encourage them to sign up to be a donor on their license should anything happen to them. Well, I was in disbelief at the amount of ignorance I was met with about donation. Some people even went as far as to say the doctors won't try to save their life in the emergency room if they know they're a donor. However, many don't know that long after the doctors have done all they can for you and pronounce you deceased, *then* the process begins of determining if you're a donor. Many times people are rushed during emergency situations and there's no time to say "Hey, he's a donor; let's not save him." I even heard some people say they wouldn't be able to have a funeral once their organs are removed; apparently these people don't know the process of preparing a body for a funeral, but I digress. It was very difficult as a dialysis patient in need of an organ, to see firsthand why the waitlist is so long, because of myths floating around many communities that deter people from saving a person's life long after they're gone. I continued to volunteer as much as my health would allow. I began making dialysis a part of my life instead of the other way around. I trained to do home dialysis to allow myself the flexibility to live a better life. I trained to hook myself up to my machine, take my own vitals, and even infuse my dialysis bags with heparin (blood thinner). I was also taught to give myself a shot in the leg every week with a medicine that helps generate red blood cells since the kidneys regulate red blood cell production. Without kidneys, less red blood cells. After nervously sweating for over an hour attempting to stick myself the first time, I delegated this responsibility to my mom. She gives shots at work as a dental hygienist to strangers, but I could imagine it has to be difficult to do for your own child in your home. I truly appreciate my mother for everything she's done and sacrificed for me while I battle this disease. I don't think we realize how much our parents give unselfishly to us from the moment we are born. Being ill helped me to see how much it takes to be a mother. I pray one day I am half the mother she is. I enrolled back in school at a local community college, not to study nursing but for human services. Nursing is no longer fun when you're the patient. Now it's very hard for me to see people in pain because it triggers my many experiences with pain and distress. It's like I feel it all over again. I know I can still impact the renal community and fulfill my purpose helping people as a social worker. School is challenging as a home dialysis patient, but I was determined to finish my degree. I had to find the right balance of classes, study time, and 13-hour treatments all while in and out of hospitals and feeling extremely tired every day. My teachers were very understanding, and I always will enroll in disability services no matter which school I go to. There are people in every school who will advocate on your behalf should you fall ill or miss class for any reason. On one occasion, my disability advocate emailed all of my teachers instead of having me worry about contacting them while I was dealing with a health scare. This type of support is very helpful when going back to school while simultaneously managing any health condition. I used to be so prideful and never would've thought I'd need disability services. But instead of being prideful about it, I welcomed the extra help to relieve some of the weight off my shoulders that came with pursuing my education. I also found a vocational rehab program that the State of Illinois offers through the Department of Human Services to help people transition off disability income by supporting them in going back to school, job training, resume building, and with many other resources and workshops. This program was very helpful for me, and I share it with everyone I know who may be able to benefit from these types of programs that most people don't always know are out there. Toward the middle of my third semester at Harper College one Thursday evening I remember eating Chipotle and watching Scandal. I began preparing for bed as I'd always done, which meant setting up my dialysis treatment, taking my vitals, evening medications, and hooking myself up to the machine ...

That is the last memory I have before waking up in a hospital bed ...

"Well, hello there. I'll give you a chance to fully wake up," the ghost said.

"Do you know where you are?"

I looked around and I said, "Yes of course, I'm in the hospital."

See, I've woken up in a hospital bed well over 100 mornings so this morning wasn't any different. Even if I didn't understand the events that transpired to get me there, this was my second home so nothing about being there felt unusual. Many of the hospital admissions all start to run together in your mind, besides some of the really traumatic ones—those you remember vividly forever. So he proceeds cautiously asking me routine neurology-test questions; which would become the daily routine over the following couple of weeks …

"Tell me what year it is."

I answered, "2014."

"Who is the current President?"

"Barack Obama."

"What's your name?"

"Leilah."

"Can you count backwards from 10?"

"10 … 9 ….8…7 …"

"Say your ABCs backwards."

I stumbled through that one; I think they ask that one to be funny because I don't know too many people who can do that one normally. The next question will haunt me for me years to come, bringing about an unimaginable amount of anxiety.

He proceeded to ask me, "Tell me what day it is?"

I said without any hesitation, "It's Friday!"

He calmly approached the bed to break the news to me that while I answered all of the other questions correctly, indicating a good sign that they can rule out brain trauma to a certain part of my brain, while others may still be affected such as long term memory meaning past events or experiences may be fuzzy or gone forever.

He went on to tell me, "Ms. Sampson, it is Tuesday." With a puzzled look I said, "No, yesterday was Thursday, today would be Friday."

You know that look on someone's face when they're listening to what you're saying but they know something you don't and they're trying to find a way to break it to you that what you're so very sure of is very wrong? Well that's the look he was giving me as he asked the most moment defining question.

"Do you know why you're here?"

I mumbled something but ultimately it dawned on me that I really didn't know why I was there; I assumed another dialysis related situation. *Hell, I don't know.*

In the most gentle voice he could muster, he sat on the bed and told me I was in the Intensive Care Unit. I'd had a really bad seizure, but luckily my mom found me in the middle of the night while I was still hooked up to my dialysis machine. I'd been placed in a medically induced coma for the last five days. There was severe swelling of my brain. He told me my blood pressure reached astronomical levels at about 200/120 whereas the normal range is 120/80. I also aspirated some vomit into my lungs which caused a mucous plug that was surgically removed. So he explained what the pain I felt breathing and the blood when I coughed was. He also said that they had to cut through my weave (disappointing, I know; I'd just gotten that hair installed) to put electrodes on my scalp to further test my brain. I underwent a series of tests such as CT scans, MRI's, chest X-Rays. I had so many questions; it was a lot to take in and frankly quite overwhelming. Scared, as I looked around to see I WAS in fact in the ICU, and my wrists were tied down in restraints. He also explained the soreness in my throat from having the tube placed to assist with breathing and that the restraints were to keep me from pulling out the tube when I thrashed about as they tried to bring me out of the coma by slowly reducing the amount of anesthesia. Just like getting put "under" for surgery, they use the same medications to induce you into a coma. It was at this moment I started to glance around and was brought back to reality. I looked down at my arms to see three IVs in each arm and one PICC line (a line that can be used for more long term treatments) in my upper arm. This was my first PICC line, and for me, it magnified the seriousness of this episode. Everyone I knew who had to get one placed was in the hospital for something very serious. I also had a hemodialysis catheter in my chest. They were able to use this catheter to give me continuous 24-hour dialysis which was easier and much stronger for someone in a coma. It allows direct access to the bloodstream for cleaning and administering medications. Over the next couple of weeks, many family and friends came to visit, sat with me, prayed with me and filled me in on the events that transpired while I was out of it. The hardest part was realizing I will always have five days of my life I can't account for. Five days that I had no control over my care or any say in what happened to me. I had no choice but to trust the people around me and healthcare team made the best decisions on my behalf. I was told I couldn't get out of bed to use the bathroom even though I could clearly see the toilet next to my bed. This was very upsetting to me because I was still in wrist restraints that were there to prevent me from attempting to get out of the bed. It was also the most humiliating experience to be awake and have nurses wipe my butt for me in bed. They informed me that because I hadn't used any motor skills in the past few days, if I attempted to get out of bed my legs would not be able to support me. They were right; the first time I started physical therapy with assistance of a nurse, my legs felt like spaghetti and I would've fallen to the floor if she wasn't holding me as I learned to walk and use my motor skills again. The same with eating: I had to start with liquids first learning how to swallow then soft foods such as apple sauce before I could gradually start eating solid foods again to ensure I wouldn't choke. Over the next couple of days, I'd still have a lot of pain when breathing and coughing up blood, but this subsided over time. I was able to "graduate" as we patients like to call it, to a regular floor. You can't just go from ICU to home. So the sooner you go down to a regular floor, the closer you are to being discharged. I'd spend a total of two weeks in the hospital recovering from "the coma." Going home didn't mean I was out of the woods; the long term mental and emotional effects from it really showed up when I was alone. I remember waking up from a mid-day nap while my mom was at work (I spent many days alone) and feeling relieved that I had this crazy dream I was very sick, in a coma, and all of my friends and family were gathered at the hospital. Then I looked over to see the cards and teddy bears, it dawned on me that it wasn't a dream; I really was in a coma. A rush of fear and anxiety came over me. This would go on for months to follow. Every time I slept and woke up, "the coma" replayed like a reoccurring nightmare I had to face every day: it wasn't a dream; it was reality. I didn't realize how traumatic the aftermath of the coma would be. My therapist and I had a lot of work ahead of us to get my anxiety under control and help me come to terms with everything that had happened. There's no going back to normal after something that traumatizing happens to you, but you can pick up the pieces and create yet another way of living, even though it feels like you're just compounding trauma on top of trauma. It won't feel that way if you properly deal with the trauma when it happens. Many of us experience traumatic situations and just think, "Well I'll get over it or it will heal itself." But trauma doesn't heal itself by avoidance. Trauma will heal itself by facing it head-on, dissecting the events, how you feel about them and reshaping the way you look at those events. For example, whenever I felt scared or anxious about the coma happening again and no one being around to find me if I had a seizure, I told myself that every time I had a seizure someone had been there so why wouldn't they be there again? God brought me through the coma. It wasn't my time to go so why would he bring me through all of that just to forsake me now? Reshaping those thoughts helped me through a lot of tough days, whereas I could've let those thoughts consume me. Now, don't get me wrong, there were days that I cried and broke down about it. Every day was a victory, and every day reminded me how blessed I am to have made it through all that I have. Many people ask me if I remember hearing or seeing anything while in the coma. I can honestly say it's more of a feeling. I experienced an overwhelming indescribable feeling of vibration and people praying for me. I truly believe in the power of prayer as a direct line to God. I say that because I know that the prayers kept me fighting to live. I felt the overwhelming amount of love and faith people were sending me. See, the thing about being in a coma is that because you're under so much medication, you don't know what's real or a hallucination. I feel in my heart, I died in that moment. I floated up, like being stuck on the ceiling and looking down surrounded by what I would describe as whipped cream, not necessarily clouds as most people would assume but it felt thicker than that. I then felt an undeniable force pushing me back down. In my heart, I know it was God.

He pushed me back to Earth, with this message: *It is not your time my child; you still have work to do.*

*T*HERE WAS A SHIFT IN THE ATMOSPHERE after my anxiety around the coma improved. I went from being terrified to be alone to regaining my power and taking control over my life. I refused to be a victim to another traumatic event. At this point, I'd experienced so many traumas in my short 20-something years of life, I could've justifiably given up. However, I think going through so much breaks people because they don't see themselves as victors, but victims. I've never enjoyed being the victim or sitting on the pity pot. I don't expect anyone to feel sorry for me or treat me like a victim. It's not about what people address you as, but what you answer to. So before anyone tries to shower me with pity, I instantly reshape the whole conversation to, "I appreciate it, but I AM blessed." You set the tone with every interaction. If you go into a situation feeling like a victim, you will be treated as such. The energy you present someone with will determine the energy they reciprocate back to you. For many years, I walked around worried about what people thought about me. Walking into a room, wondering if they could tell I was sick. Wondering if they knew I was on dialysis. Did they think any less of me? Was I considered weak and needed their pity? But then I have to remember everything I'd not only gone through, but OVERCOME. I now feel an electricity of confidence in any situation because I *know* I'm the strongest person in the room. See, there's a difference in needing others to validate you and you validating yourself. I stopped looking for people to tell or show me how I should feel about myself. I stopped waiting for their energy to dictate how I moved. I found that when you meet people with strong, confident energy, you force them to rise to meet your energy level. Like smiling at someone—it's rare that they don't feel compelled to smile back. When I started changing the way I viewed myself, the world, and my situation, I noticed the universe changed the way it responded to me. I started eating better, because let's face it, no one is perfect when it comes to diet, and a renal diet is truly an uphill battle—one you can only take one meal at a time, along with many restrictions and adjustments you have to make. But I knew that in order to prepare my spirit and my body for receiving the ultimate Gift of Life (a kidney), I had to be actively trying to get into the best shape of my life. I will admit, my monthly blood work at my dialysis center weren't that great in previous years. Even on dialysis, which is only a treatment for kidney disease and not a cure, your blood isn't being cleaned to the effectiveness that it would if you actually had functioning kidneys. Coupled with poor diet and a body in turmoil, these levels can cause atrophy (death) to certain organs. I know firsthand the effects of a dangerous phosphorus and parathyroid hormone level which led to me having a total parathyroidectomy A parathyroidectomy is the removal of four parathyroid glands due to atrophy. The kidneys regulate so many things in your body like phosphorus levels. Controlling phosphorus is a huge struggle for many patients, because it means you have to limit many foods that you enjoy daily, such as dairy, canned and processed foods, and the list goes on. It feels almost impossible to limit phosphorus intake, so many patients like me, just give up instead of fighting with the long list and food labels. But, I was determined to make a change; at this point my life depended on it. I survived an almost-fatal seizure and God renewed my fight. It was like having my batteries recharged. I was full of fight and life. There was nothing stopping me from receiving this kidney if I could help it. My therapist offered an amazing guided meditation class every week that introduced me to a new way of harnessing my energy and thoughts to visualize the life I wanted for myself. She'd guide me in visualizing the flow of life through my heart. I'd then visualize holding my kidney in either hand. I always visualized it in my left hand. When you receive a transplanted kidney they put it in the front of your body, either on the left or right side, so it directly connects with your bladder. Unlike your native kidneys which sit in your back, the transplanted kidneys aren't harvested with long enough veins and arteries to reach your bladder if they were placed in the back. Meditation helped me to slow down my thoughts and just have a clear, blank mind for that moment. My thoughts were constantly racing with scheduling surgeries, work, dialysis, medications, appointments, volunteering and just the day-to-day business of life. Overwhelming is an understatement. I've never drowned in water before but I know how it feels to drown in life. Meditation was a catalyst for renewing my spirituality.

It was at this point in my life when I renewed my belief in Christianity. I began attending church again. I found comfort and hope in the Holy Bible. Many of the scriptures got me through tough times; just reading them brought me so much peace. I'd never sat down on my own and read the Bible. I now have a study Bible that breaks down theology (the study of religious beliefs). I, like many people, have always felt overwhelmed by how large the Bible is. But I recommend purchasing a study Bible to anyone interested in learning how to dissect the Bible and apply it to your life. In church, my pastor led us in thanking Jesus (the son of God) for how much we'd already overcome and in advance for blessings we hadn't received yet. I'd thank Jesus and God for delivering me through so much and for a kidney I hadn't received yet. I truly believe you can speak things into existence. Every day, I'd claim, "By His Stripes I AM Healed." I envisioned and dreamt about my new kidney in my body and how it would feel, what the call would sound like, when it would happen. I had a gut feeling the call would happen in the middle of the night. Every night I'd sleep with my phone on loud, so I didn't miss any calls in case it was the hospital with a kidney offer. This brought about a lot of sleepless nights and anxiety. My biggest fear was my phone dying or not hearing the call, only to see the missed opportunity in the morning. But every night I went to bed knowing I was a day closer to receiving that call whenever God saw fit. In the morning I'd be met with disappointment, day after day, week after week, month after month. Four and a half years of disappointment. I'd look in the mirror and didn't recognize myself. My skin had gotten darker and riddled with acne from a weakened immune system that causes bacteria to easily infect your pores. Scars. The scars. So many scars. My once perfect athletic-firm body was now a science project and I felt like a living version of the game Operation. Who is this woman? Who is this person staring back at me? This can't be the same person who was so young and ambitious with her whole life planned out. This woman was somebody I didn't know, like waking up to a stranger in your house every morning. Strange equipment. Strange tubes. Strange life. None of it made sense. Looking into my own eyes in the mirror like portals to my soul, I'd ask myself, "How did you get here? Will you live to see another day? Of course you will, just keep fighting girl. You made it this far. Do you know what you've overcome? You are invincible. You are superwoman. Never forget."

Then one August day, the hospital called. The heart palpitations that came from seeing that number on my Caller ID were as strong right then as they were the first day—and every time they called. Over the course of four and a half years they've called to tell me *You have a match! Sorry, you DON'T currently have any potential donors. We need more tests completed. We need more documentation. There's an issue with your insurance. We need more tests. Your test results look fine. Your test results don't look so good. We're sending you for more tests. We're sending you to a Specialist. We need more tests. You have a match! Sorry, you don't have any potential donors currently. You have another match. Sorry, you don't have a match.* So the amount of disappointment outweighed the good news whenever that number showed up on my phone. But this call was slightly different. The Transplant Nurse on the other end said, "Ms. Sampson we'd like you to come in for another test. Our records indicate you haven't completed your cardiac testing. We still need a stress test and echocardiogram." I thought, *what the hell is the point of me running down there to do another d@%n test? I've done enough.* They explained to me that without this test they were placing me on "HOLD." I was furious. "Hold" on the transplant list means that if a kidney offer came up that very moment you wouldn't be considered for it. All of your tests needed to be up-to-date at all times, so they know you were cleared and surgery ready. So I finally scheduled the appointment, completed the tests, and everything looked good. I was back listed to "ACTIVE" status. I thought about all the potential offers I could've missed in the two weeks it took to schedule the tests and have the results reviewed by a transplant doctor. It was a nerve wracking two weeks to say the least. My mother kept reassuring me, that I had to be close to receiving the kidney offer; there was no other reason they'd call with such urgency to get me down to complete the test *and* go to such extreme measures by placing me on hold. At the time, I was so riddled with disappointment from these transplant program calls, as bad as I wanted the kidney, I just didn't want to see their number show up on my phone unless they were calling to offer me a kidney. Suddenly, the roles reversed. As I marinated on their urgency to get me in for updated tests, the more anxious I became. The more I called them. Every other day, "Hey are you sure I have everything completed? Are you sure I'm Active"? And each time with amazing patience they'd say, "Yes Ms. Sampson we have everything. You're all set."

So, remember at the very beginning when I went in for a transplant evaluation with my family, to test for donors? Well, I was scheduled for another evaluation, except this one was different. I was alone with a transplant nurse and he proceeded to tell me that I was, in fact, close to the top of the deceased donor list. With four and a half years' time accrued on the list and all of this preparation, I could receive the call at any moment. He continued, telling me to have my phone on at all times, an overnight hospital bag packed in my car, and to stay as healthy as possible. If you're in the hospital or sick at the time of the call for a kidney offer you may not be eligible for the kidney. He also explained that I have the legal right to accept or deny any kidney that is 'offered' to me. Of course, I'm thinking, *"Now why in the HELL would someone refuse A KIDNEY?"* See, here's the thing: not every kidney harvested for donation is in perfect condition and the same goes for the deceased donor. The nurse informed me that I may be offered a Donor after Cardiac Death kidney; this means the kidney was harvested after the donor's heart stopped either in the emergency room or after the family decided to "pull the plug." I was told DCD Kidneys have poor outcomes. *So why would anyone accept that one,* I wondered He then informed me he wouldn't recommend I sign a consent form to be considered for an Expanded Criteria Donor kidney, which is typically an elder person over the age of 60. They do not recommend young people receive this type of kidney because they typically do not last very long, requiring that person to go back on dialysis and need another transplant. As of December 2014, the Kidney Allocation Program was modified so young patients on the Kidney Transplant List are considered for kidneys from young deceased donors. I was ecstatic to know I met the criteria for this new modification so if a kidney was offered to me it would most likely come from a younger donor—with hopes of that kidney providing me with a longer dialysis-free life.

They say a little knowledge can be harmful. I spent every day at work researching scholarly journals on potential transplant donor outcomes. All I knew was I wanted the best possible kidney to provide me with the best possible outcome. But I had so many questions: What if they offer me a DCD Kidney? Should I take it? I mean, isn't any kidney better than NO KIDNEY?? I'd spent almost five years fighting for my life and looking death in the face on numerous occasions, so would I really have the courage to deny an offer if it were presented to me? I was advised to consult not the transplant nephrologist but my own nephrologist, who'd managed all of my care on dialysis. At one of my monthly dialysis appointments I asked him, "Dr. Najafi, what are your thoughts on DCD Kidneys. I was told to ask your opinion? Should I take it if presented to me?" His response was simple: "You take any kidney they offer you." He continued, "Any kidney is better than what you have now (nothing at all). You're better off taking your chances and praying for the best." This only made things even more complicated. I wanted to know in some magical way, no matter what time of day or night the offer was presented, I'd make a clear and sound decision. I wrote Post-it notes reminding myself not to accept any DCD kidneys and a list of all of the people I needed to contact such as my therapist, family, and work. Just in case in the heat of the moment I was too excited to think straight. As the days passed, my anxiety grew. I just couldn't believe they'd get me all worked up and have me driving around with a packed bag in my car every day since they didn't even know when I'd get the call. All they kept telling me was, *it could be today, next week, or six months from now. We just don't know.* I had no other choice but to wait. I found solace in the Word of the Holy Bible and church. I'd waited over four years; the long stretch was over but it felt even more intense because I knew it was close, I just didn't know when. My therapist, Monica, suggested I continue to envision the kidney in my body and make room in my life for it. My kidney needed to know it had a safe, welcoming, and loving place with me. I continued meditating and creating boundaries with people in my life who were absorbing the energy I needed to receive this kidney. It's amazing how people can see you struggling and dealing with your own battles and yet they still expect you to overextend yourself. But it's solely up to you to freely give that energy away. I had to realize that we all will leave this Earth alone. You are the only person responsible for protecting your energy, your happiness, and your body. It took many years on dialysis before I figured this out. I dealt with plenty of disappointments from people and being manipulated, but that's not what this book is about. I prefer to keep the negativity to a minimum. I will not give any of my energy back to old situations or people who may have hurt me or let me down by giving them a page in my book. I want people to take away that no matter how many people hurt or manipulate you; the choice is always yours to allow it in or not. Along with creating boundaries, I needed a safe clean space to recover. I reached out to my aunt who is a retired nurse, lives close to my hospital, has no pets, and lives on the first floor of a condo. Who better to help me recover after surgery? She agreed to let me come stay post-transplant surgery. I went to her house sat in the room and prayed in the space. We put together a bed my dad ordered, cleaned the room; I knew it was perfect. I laid across the bare bed, no sheets, no pillows, just a mattress and I looked up at the vent on the ceiling. I said aloud, "You're going to lay in this bed recovering from transplant surgery with your new kidney and look up at this vent and remember you claimed it all."

ON A CHILLY MID-DECEMBER NIGHT after hanging out with a friend from work I fell asleep around 10 p.m. Nothing about this night seemed any different. This night would change my life forever. I woke up around 12:30 a.m. to see I had several missed calls, voicemails, and text messages. The missed calls were from an inner city number that looked pretty familiar. The text message from my mom read "LEILAH NW (Northwestern Hospital) IS TRYING TO CALL YOU." Before even calling her back, I checked the voicemail from the unidentified number. I was nervous, excited, but scared because *what if I was too late?* What if they were calling me with a kidney offer and I was two hours too late? Did they just call the next person on the list and I'd missed my chance? The thought of my biggest fear being a reality made me sick for a moment. The voicemail was from a nurse on the transplant team calling to inform me that they indeed had a potential kidney offer for me and to call her back as soon as I got the message. But then I noticed she'd left two more voicemails, each with a little more urgency in her voice to call her back. Before I could get through all of the messages, I called her back praying I didn't miss my chance of receiving the Gift of Life. She told me that I was next up on the list to receive the next available organ, although there were about five other people listed at different hospitals who were being considered for the offer as well. So technically it wasn't mine, but they needed to know legally did I accept the offer if they do decide it would be mine. She began telling me the specifics of the donor; he was a young male about my age (26) died from an apparent suicide. That was hard to hear. It was unfortunate that he lost his battle with depression and was successful in committing suicide. I thought about my own suicide attempt. I was blessed to have not been successful and climb out of depression. I know I would've kept attempting without the help I received on the psych floors. As if that wasn't bad enough, she proceeded to tell me that it was a DCD (Donor after Cardiac Death) kidney. I couldn't believe my luck. What the ...? I knew time was ticking and they needed to know my decision, but I had to slow them down. I asked, *what exactly does that mean?* All of my research and all of my notes didn't mean a thing in that very moment.

She told me that the problem with this kidney is that it took a "hit."

Confused, I asked, "What exactly do you mean, a hit?"

She said, "Well, sometimes when a kidney is without blood flow for some time, it can cause part of the organ to start to die." I was speechless. She then put us on a conference call with a transplant nephrologist who was on call at the time. He went over the logistics of the kidney from the records he had and I asked him, "Do you think I should take it? Do you think it has a good chance of working well?"

He said, "To be honest with you, I think you should take it; it's a young viable kidney and the history of the donor looks good."

I still had a lot to think about, but no time to; they needed an answer. I mulled it over. In my head I could hear my dialysis doctor's words telling me, "You take whatever they offer you." I thought, well they wouldn't offer me a kidney they didn't think would work. In that moment, I closed my eyes and said... "YES, I'LL TAKE IT!" We disconnected from the on-call nephrologist and the nurse proceeded to read me a bunch of legal documents. But my excitement wouldn't let any of it permeate my brain. She quickly reminded me that it still wasn't mine officially. But, even in the face of uncertainty I *knew* it was my time. I got on my knees and prayed to God. I said to Him, "Please let this one be for me. I know you've heard my prayers, seen my efforts, and felt my willingness to fight."

This kidney needed a fighter and I was up for the challenge. I'd proven myself in more ways than one that I was not easily broken. The nurse assured me that if I had any questions I could call her back directly, but in the meantime I should come down to the hospital to get checked in. I lived 45 minutes away so it was best that I made my way there to get prepped, in case they decided the kidney would go to me. I grabbed the bag I had packed in my car and started rushing around my room throwing more stuff in it like a crazy woman. I called my parents, but I'd known for months that I wanted to have this operation alone. Next, I called my therapist, Monica. Even though it was the middle of the night she knew it was THEE call. She'd always assured me I could call her when THEE call came through, no matter the time. I expressed to her I was nervous and didn't have the heart to tell my family they couldn't share this moment with me. Some may see it as selfish or harsh. However, I'd had numerous surgeries and although I appreciated my parents for being there, their anxiety was too much to handle before going under the knife. Sometimes people's presence does more harm than good. I understand it's hard for parents to hide the level of fear they have about their child going under the knife. Many times you hear horror stories of parents kissing their child goodbye, watching them whisked away by nurses and doctors only to never make it out of surgery and that's the last image the parents have of their child. I knew I needed to do this alone in the most calm and peaceful manner for my spirit and body to accept this kidney. My therapist encouraged me to just tell them, but I couldn't handle their emotions at the time. I needed to reserve my energy for myself. I couldn't expend any energy answering questions from family or friends. Especially since I wasn't sure if it was even mine. I called a coworker and by this time it was 3a.m. She answered a little taken aback; I assumed she'd been sleeping. I apologized for waking her but I explained to her I'd just received the kidney call and I needed her to give me a ride to the hospital. She agreed. I showered and grabbed my packed bag. I let my mom know I was going to the hospital but it wasn't finalized and I'd let her know if it was official. I left the house in a bit of a tizzy. I freaked out the whole drive to my coworker's house. I screamed, I cried, but more praying than anything. I prayed for safe travels. I prayed that I wouldn't get down there and be turned away. I've known people to get the kidney call four or more times, only to be sent home and the kidney given to someone else. I couldn't fathom that kind of devastation. When I arrived at my coworker's complex, I left my car in her parking lot and we hopped in hers. The whole way to downtown Chicago from the northern suburbs we chatted, laughed, and she wished me well as she dropped me off at the emergency room. I was told by the transplant nurse to check-in at the ER desk. I told the secretary I was there for a kidney transplant. She was so excited for me. I felt a bit confused as to why I was going in through the ER, but the secretary was so prepared and thorough with getting me all signed in and directing me to the elevators up to the transplant floor, it was obvious: this was routine. The best way to describe the feeling is like being a member of a secret club and being let in through the back door. I was granted instant access to the transplant floor, but the access is well deserved. Everybody there knows what you've been through and what it takes to reach that very moment. It's like defeating Bowser to save Princess Peach in the video game Super Mario Brothers. I defeated all levels and overcame many obstacles to make it to Transplant Victory. I got on the steel patient-transport-only elevators, jumping around recording videos of the entire journey upstairs. Stepping off the elevator onto the transplant floor was unlike anything I could've ever imagined; it was unforgettable. Everyone (nurses, doctors, surgeons, and assistants) welcomes you with open arms. Everyone wants to know your story (as if they haven't heard a million "I survived" stories). But the empathy is so genuine; they feel for you because they understand the reality of waiting for an organ. I was shown to my room, given a gown, and told to relax because it'd be awhile before they heard anything about the status of The Kidney. At this point, it was 5 o'clock in the morning. I was instructed not to eat anything in case we were moving forward with the surgery. I was entirely too anxious to sleep from the moment I received THEE CALL. Next, the nurse came in to ask admission questions. I've always hated this part of the hospital stay, oh, but this time was different. I was happy to report to her, there'd been no changes in my medications or health. I hadn't been sick recently or hospitalized. Of course, you'll make yourself look like the prime candidate to receive this organ. But they do a full set of blood work to see for themselves just how "good" you claim your health has been. While I continued to wait, I called my Sister in Christ, MiMi. She always assured me that whenever I got THEE CALL, she'd be there, day or night. I knew early on, I wanted her to be there with me. There are people in your life who bring you closer to God, and peace in times of unrest. She is the epitome of a beautiful soul. No, I'm not saying she is perfect. However, she's been in my life for over a decade and has remained just as genuine and faithful to God as the first day I met her. When I was in spiritual turmoil, I knew I could turn to the women of the Rudy Family to comfort my spirit and provide me with clarity. God used them as a vessel for me to get closer to Him and renew my faith. She came to the transplant floor about 10 a.m. I was ecstatic to see her. Any anxiety I had immediately turned into excitement. The transplant doctor came in to inform me that the kidney had been harvested from the deceased donor. It was en route to the Gift of Hope Headquarters about 45 minutes outside of Chicago to undergo more testing. The Gift of Hope Organ &

Tissue Donor Network manages all donor organs in the Illinois area and receives all of the potential recipients' blood each month, analyze it, and enter the information such as blood type into a national database managed by UNOS (United Network for Organ Sharing). To my understanding, this database automatically matches recipients and donors. The kidney then goes from the Gift of Hope to whichever hospital the next compatible patient is "listed" for donation. I was told there were about five other patients listed at other hospitals who were in "competition" for the kidney with me I didn't know if they'd been ruled out (based on blood type, health, age, etc.) or turned down the kidney I was so desperately praying for. The transplant surgeon came in to speak with me about the kidney. He reiterated that the kidney took a "hit." As if I needed another reminder. Remember, some kidneys, before being harvested, go without blood or oxygen which could cause damage to it. So I asked him, *what does this mean? Are you saying that I can't have this one?* He told me they'd do another biopsy on it and run some tests, to see if they felt it was viable enough to move forward with transplant. At this point, I'm still not completely sure if its technically mine or not. I think he already knew they'd give it to me but wanted to "test the waters" to see if I was willing to accept it and the potential risks that may come along with a high-risk kidney. It didn't take long before he came back in and said, "CONGRATS! It's yours, and we're ready to move forward with the transplant!" MiMi and I freaked out with excitement. The surgeon continued talking to me about the risks of surgery and double checking my history. I began telling him how I fought so hard for this moment! I had given up drinking pop, juice, and sweets. I'd only been drinking water, praying, yoga, meditation, volunteering, and had gone back to work. I also shared my story with him about how I became ill in college while studying to become a nurse. He insisted that I go back to school and become a nurse or a doctor. I explained to him that after being a patient and my own nurse I couldn't handle seeing patients in pain because I know firsthand what the pain was like. I told him I'd have way too much empathy. He stopped me right there. He said, "There's no such thing as too much empathy. As doctors we struggle with not having enough empathy for our patients because we don't know what it's like to go through dialysis or a transplant." He was right. I then said, "Well besides, I'd be on immunosuppressant drugs the rest of my life, which makes me highly susceptible to infections and the last place I need to be is in a hospital around sick people." He agreed and followed it up with "Yea that makes more sense." This reminded me of a professor I had in college. She'd been a pediatric oncology (cancer) nurse for many years. She told us how she became attached to a lot of her patients so she'd hug them and get really close to them. One of her patients she'd taken care of for many years had a bad virus that she wasn't informed about. She is now partially deaf. She lost all of her hearing in her right ear. She told us how much her family resented her for caring about those patients so much so that she put her own health at risk. Hearing that story further solidified in my mind that being an immunocompromised nurse in a hospital wasn't for me. I prefer to help from a more social and philanthropic standpoint.

"You. Can. Never. Have. Too. Much. Empathy."

Before he left the room, he asked me "Which side would you like the Kidney Transplanted on?" It didn't take me long, but I knew I wanted it on the left. Pointing to my lower left side I said, "Yea right here looks good to me!" Maybe because at the time my current dialysis catheter was on my right side, but I'd been making room through meditation and focusing my energy on that side of my body to house this beautiful Gift of Life. He marked my left side with a surgical marker and that sealed the deal. MiMi brought her Bible and a special "Transplant Prayer" she'd found online. See, this is the type of support system you need in your life. Someone who comes prepared to speak life and prayer over you before surgery. I was so grateful for her in that moment. I knew through her words and assurance in her voice that it was already written in God's Plan for me to receive this kidney. We followed it up with an *Amen*. Even the nurse was moved to tears. It was the most beautiful prayer and moment I could've imagined. Under the curtain I could see the shoes and hear the voices of the nurses in the hallway with the bed ready to take me down to THEE Kidney Transplant Surgery Floor. It was actually HAPPENING. I couldn't believe it. I was more excited than nervous. The Surgeon asked, "Aren't you nervous?" I said, "Absolutely NOT!" I'd waited four years and

10 months on dialysis, dreamt of this moment, prayed for this moment, meditated on this moment, and nearly died waiting for this moment. I just wanted it to happen. I couldn't wait any longer. MiMi and I waited in the pre-operation area where more nurses hooked me up to monitoring machines. Then, an anesthesiologist came back to talk to me about my past history with anesthesia which wasn't very extensive because I'd never had a problem with it during my many surgeries over the years. He also gave me "something to relax me" before they took me back. I was used to this whole process, but for some reason I didn't feel scared like the other surgeries. I felt so at peace and excited. I hugged MiMi goodbye as they wheeled me to the back. She said she was going home and would come back in a few days. That was the last thing I remembered before taking a good 'ole trip to la-la land. I was grateful she was there with me for so many hours. My pre-transplant moment was exactly how I'd envisioned it: peaceful, prayerful, full of laughter and love.

Philippians 4:6
"Do not fret or have anxiety about anything, but with prayer, petition and proper thanksgiving make your wants and needs known to God." (The Holy Bible)

MIMI WROTE THIS SCRIPTURE AND OTHERS DOWN for me on a little Post-it note that I hung on my mirror for months prior to the kidney transplant. This scripture brought me so much comfort many days as I grew weary waiting. I read it every day and it reminded me not to worry, but just continue to thank God for past, present, and future blessings. I'd cast all of my fears onto Him. In doing so, I was able to push forward and continue my day-to-day responsibilities to stay alive and have a good quality of life. I tell people: you don't need to memorize the entire Bible; you can just find one or two scriptures that resonate with you and every time you read it; you find strength and peace. I never would've thought I'd return to church or renew my faith in Christianity. I'd been hurt by members of the church before, like many of us have. The church I attend here in Chicago is about giving "New Life" to those who'd been hurt by previous churches or people. It's a church of second chances to get it (your faith) right. Also, when you become chronically ill, your faith in God is often put to the test. I felt so angry with God, as did many of my family members. *How could He do this to me? I was on the "right path." How could He put me through so much hurt and pain like this? What did I do to deserve His wrath?* I stopped believing there was a God, at times. I always thought He was supposed to supply our every need and not cause us any harm. I was raised Catholic so it's not like I'd never been in church. But you see, you can show up to church every day since the day you were born and not receive what is being taught. That was me. I was there physically, but I didn't understand any of it. I'd tried again when I made my way to college. I went to one of the Baptist churches in Tuskegee. Man, that church was lively. It fed my soul. But still, I don't think I could apply and understand "The Word" of the Holy Bible like I do now. It really took for me to be broken all the way down and gasping for air before I reached out to the only lifeline that would save me: Christianity. Sure, God lives in all of us, but Christianity is the vessel for ME that brought me closer to my faith in God. This book is not to push anyone toward Christianity. This book is about my journey and finding my faith in Christianity and God is a part of that journey. I truly believe everyone will find their way to God—in their own time. I had to surrender to Him and kneel at His feet before He knew I was ready to receive the ultimate Gift of Life. It was only through Christ that I was built back up from the ashes of despair and disappointment. It was only through Christ that I was shown how to love life again and thank Him for life and His blessings. Things don't just happen at random. God has a plan for all of us. Sometimes, we get caught up in our wants and needs that we don't stop to listen to Him and the universe telling us which way to go. If you just be still you will find all the answers you need. He instilled in me at a young age a deep passion of concern for others. I always felt I was created to be used. But what I didn't know was how.

I was no stranger to opening my eyes in the Intensive Care Unit. Oh, but this time. This time I was made whole again. Like the last puzzle piece to a 1,000-piece puzzle that took seven years to reconstruct. I woke up to a nurse telling me that if I felt any pain to push the button in my hand. I was drowsy still from the anesthesia so I didn't really hear much, but I definitely felt the pain she was talking about. I pushed the button. It infused a dose of Morphine through my IV and lights out. I'm not sure how many times I'd done this before I woke up to see my parents sitting next to me. It was dark outside so apparently it was evening, by the time I fully came to. I went into surgery around 12 p.m. The surgery usually takes around three to four hours. They have kidney transplants down to a science now. Northwestern Medicine transplants over five kidneys a week. I knew I was in good hands. The surgeon came in to tell me the surgery was a success. He also informed me that I had a Foley catheter in my "*you know what*" that went up to the bladder that was held in place by an inflated balloon as not to slip out and catch my urine. Wow. Urine. I hadn't heard that word in a long time in regard to *me*. I hadn't urinated in over four years since I had my native kidneys removed in October of 2011. I'd still have the sensation of running to the bathroom to pee, especially in the morning after waking up, only to release a drop or two. That was extremely disappointing. For some idiotic reason every time I expected a full stream of pee. It reminded me every day how much I'd lost. I'm not exactly sure what the drops were but my nephrologist assured me it wasn't urine since I no longer had kidneys.

The surgeon also explained to me that my bladder was a muscle; without use in over four years it had shrunk, and would take some time to get stronger and expand. The Foley would alleviate any pressure on the bladder over the next few weeks. Next, he explained the Jackson-Pratt drain that was sutured to my left side, right above the 20 staples that enclosed the kidney. This drain collected all of the blood and fluids that accumulated around the kidney. The nurse had to squeeze the grenade-shaped ball at the end and stretch the tubing every few hours to move any clots along. I felt a strange and kind of painful sensation between my legs. It was urine exiting my body through the catheter into a collection bag. I'd measure urine output over the next few months to help determine how well the kidney was functioning. Eventually the pain would subside, but it was still a foreign feeling I'd just have to get used to because it was totally worth it. I dozed off and woke up the next day to the nurses telling me I needed to start moving around. The worst thing you want to do post-surgery is lie still. You need to start getting your blood flowing to all of your extremities to prevent blood clots and preventing any mucous build up in your lungs. The nurse got me up to the recliner chair very slowly because she knew the amount of pain I was about to experience. She told me to hit the pain pump before we began. First, she moved my legs then told me on the count of three she'd sit me up and let my legs dangle off the side of the bed. I took a deep breath and on three, I let out the biggest howl of pain when she thrusted me forward. I don't think the morphine helped at all, but if it did I'd hate to experience that kind of movement without it. I sat up in the chair for a couple of hours attached to an IV pole with numerous tubes and drains coming out of every part of my body. After a few hours in the recliner, texting friends and family, returning phones calls, and updating on Instagram and Facebook that I was out of surgery and doing well; it was time to stand up. I needed to take a walk around the ICU floor before I could get transferred down to the transplant floor to complete my recovery before going home. The standing up part wasn't as bad as the initial move out of bed. The nurse was so excited to have *a patient walking.* In ICU, as you can imagine, most aren't well enough to get out of bed, let alone walk. As we walked past the other rooms, many of the patients were on breathing machines with numerous tubes over their faces. That was me at one point in time. However, to be on the other side of that type of battle was a blessing; I had come out victorious. After we took our lap around the unit, it was official: I passed the test to get transferred to the transplant floor. The nurse was going to call the transport team when I shouted, "We're walking down there!" She was so ecstatic. She packed up my things and paraded me around the unit exclaiming, "My first ever transplant patient to WALK down to the transplant floor!" I asked her to take a few pictures to document that amazing moment—of course I had to post them. It was a slow walk, but I made it. Everyone down there was just as excited to see me walking onto the floor. I guess I didn't realize the magnitude of them seeing a 48-hour post kidney transplant patient *walking* from floor to floor. Trust me, this wasn't the hardest thing I'd overcome. I think your body is just waiting for that organ to kick in and give you back all the strength and energy you'd been missing. I'm sure it was a combination of receiving the organ and my adrenaline from my dreams and prayers finally coming to fruition. After a few days on the transplant floor, managing pain, monitoring kidney function through blood work and urine tests, and learning all about my new transplant medications, I was told that I'd be going home. The worst place to be post-transplant or any surgery is in the hospital. The hospital sees so many cases of the worst bacteria, viruses, and diseases you could easily catch a nosocomial (hospital-acquired) infection through the vents or medical professionals going from room to room. A few friends and family members came by to see me both at the hospital and home. I was grateful for the outpour of love I received in person, through calls/texts, and social media posts. My aunt Brenda came to pick me up from the entrance of the hospital. She refused to step foot in a hospital after all she'd seen as a retired nurse of 20-plus years. As arranged months before, I was headed to her home just 10 to 15 minutes away to begin my healing process. I couldn't wait to lay in that bed we put together, in the space I claimed, and look up at that vent. I knew in that moment that I had prayed all of this into existence. I was determined to take a shower and my aunt wasn't going to let me lay around. She told me if I wanted to shower, I needed to put up the shower rod myself. So there I was, four days out from transplant and multiple drains hanging out of my body (because I still had my dialysis catheter in my stomach), putting up a shower rod and curtain. I don't know if it's an undeniable force of strength and perseverance or if I just do dumb stuff sometimes. There's nothing like a nice hot shower after surgery and a week in the hospital; it was completely worth the nuisance of the putting up the curtain. After two days, I noticed a decrease in my urine output, increase in my blood pressure, and a slight cough. I called the 24-hour transplant helpline to speak to a nurse about how I was feeling. She told me to immediately come back to the hospital to the ER. I told my aunt and of course with her experience as a nurse, she knew how important it was to get me back to the hospital. Even though she didn't like hospitals, she stayed with me in the Emergency room all night. After running the usual tests: blood, urine analysis, and chest X-ray. The transplant surgeon on call came to speak with me. He informed me that my hemoglobin and platelet levels increased. I knew from dialysis: low hemoglobin meant low red blood cell production, and that is never good. He also informed me that he saw a trace of pneumonia in one of my lungs on the chest X-ray. But what confused me was the high platelet level. I didn't know what platelets did or how the level being high affected anything. Furthermore, I wanted to know *why* this random level increased. He said it'd be best they bring me back in to the hospital while they figure it out. Of course he feared the worst with a newly transplanted kidney: rejection. No sooner had I left the transplant floor, I was back. They began treating me for the pneumonia, but unfortunately it still continued to progress. I felt like I was drowning (that seems to be a common theme in this book, huh?) in mucous, and my lungs were tight. I struggled to breathe minute to minute. This was the worst bout of pneumonia I'd ever had. I'm sure being immunocompromised didn't help. After addressing the pneumonia issue, we still needed to tackle the hemoglobin and platelet problem. The transplant nephrologist came to see me and suggested that I'd need a blood transfusion. I immediately freaked out and started crying. I've had a few blood transfusions before. I was over the thought of getting someone else's blood—especially after a whole organ transplant. When you receive any type of blood or tissue from someone else, you receive the donor's antigens. The antibodies that exist naturally in your body to fight off anything foreign will attack donor antigens. The last thing you want to do is add *another* person's antigens into the mix with a freshly transplanted organ that came with its own set of antigens. I'd read about transplant patients rejecting their organ because of receiving a blood transfusion. I asked the doctors if this was safe and if rejection was possible. They agreed that it was possible, but they said I'd lose the kidney if my hemoglobin level stayed as low as it was. I was faced with a decision I felt so discouraged to make. I'd risk rejecting my kidney for the transfusion or risk rejecting the kidney because of lack of blood flow to it. Again, What.The.F. I thought getting this kidney was supposed to alleviate this kind of mess. But of course, things are never simple and easy for me.

MiMi came back up to the hospital to console me. I mulled over the decision, talked to a few more doctors, prayed about it and cried some more, but eventually I decided to take my chances with the transfusion. I watched them hook me up to the blood, and all I could do was pray that the blood did not cause a rejection episode. I received two units of blood to bring my hemoglobin levels back up to normal with no signs of rejection from the transfusions. However, the high platelet level did suggest some form of rejection or reoccurrence of my kidney disease (FSGS). Fearing my disease was returning, they told me I needed to start Plasmapheresis as soon as possible. I'd already known what it was because typically you receive this treatment before transplant if you have enough time to prepare. This treatment "washes" your blood of your antibodies by drawing your blood from your body through a machine, which separates out your plasma and puts it back. Now, I wasn't freaking out from this treatment *as much* because, as you can see, this treatment would be very helpful in preventing rejection or reoccurrence. The part I wasn't too happy about was that this type of treatment is similar to hemodialysis, which requires direct access to your blood through a major artery. I'd never had a fistula or graft (permanent dialysis access). I needed to have one placed immediately in my chest. The appointment was made in interventional radiology before I could even object to it. I asked my transplant nephrologist, Dr. Shetty, "Be honest with me. Can I beat all of this?" Meaning, *will I lose this kidney and go back on dialysis or even worse will I die?* Because the way my body felt, I wouldn't have been surprised if she'd told me that it wasn't looking too good. Instead, she reassured me that they had plenty of treatments to try before even considering having me go back on dialysis. She also reassured me that we caught the pneumonia early enough and started the antibiotics right away so it would clear up completely in a couple of weeks. I just needed to keep coughing up the mucous and breathing deeply to break up any mucous that might be settling in my lower lungs. I was transported down to interventional radiology. I told the nurse this was my sixth chest catheter and I'd had some terrible experiences. She told me she was a great mixologist and would ensure that I had a nice cocktail of sedation medicines to "take the edge off." I laughed and immediately felt better. This time was no different from all the other chest catheters placed in my heart. I could probably do the procedure on myself. They clean you up with cold soap, numb the breast tissue with about eight shots of Lidocaine. After that, all you feel is your blood running down your chest to your armpit, from the scalpel that cuts a slit in your skin to access the artery. Next, the doctor slides the tubing into the artery that leads to your heart. Flush with saline. Suture it up with stitches and 45 minutes later you have a new access. The pain after the Lidocaine wears off is the worst part about the whole thing. You don't want to move any part of your upper body, especially not your neck. The pain from having a tube jammed in your heart is a completely different level of pain. I came back up from interventional radiology to my parents awaiting my return.

So there I was with a Foley catheter, chest catheter, 20

staples, a J-P drain, pneumonia, two blood transfusions, daily plasmapheresis and my current PD (home dialysis) catheter fighting to keep this kidney.

The nights were long and tough. My thoughts began to spiral out of control. The pain all over my body kept me up all night. I couldn't lie on any side except my back. I was up to urinate every 20 minutes, which was a blessing to finally make urine—that meant the kidney was still functioning. I had to keep telling myself, "Remember when you didn't pee? Be grateful. Even if you never get another wink of sleep." I think after not sleeping for two to three days at a time, your mind becomes a playground for depression to sneak in and have its way with you. I'd lie in the dark all day—and didn't want any more visitors at this point. Things had gotten bad. MiMi put me in touch with a pastor she knew who comforted me as well. She gave me some scriptures to read, but the best advice she gave me was to rest. REST. I needed to just rest in the Lord. I needed to let Him take over. I'd done all I could do at this point. There was no more fighting to be done. I just needed to trust with unrelenting faith that He would see me through this. Besides, he'd brought me all the way through the transplant there was no way He'd forsake me now. The pastor continued to check on me daily, reminding me to stay strong and continue to rest. My mom came almost every day after work. She'd always fall asleep, but her presence was comforting and distracted me from the terrible thoughts and depression I was dealing with. I don't think anyone knew just how deeply depressed I was. You see, when they notified me the night of the call that I had a potential donor, I asked them "Well, how did he die?" The nurse told me he dealt with depression for a while and decided to end his life. Stunned, I felt terrible. However, my life depended on this organ. What I didn't realize is how much his depression would live on through his organ and become a part of me. Many diseases are caused by stress, because anxiety can move from being an emotional struggle to manifesting physically. Everything we eat, observe, and feel becomes a part of us. I, too, deal with depression and attempted suicide. Depression is something you will battle with all of your life; it doesn't go away with a magic pill or a magic kidney. All I could think about was his family. I prayed they find comfort and peace. It hurt that while I was celebrating a new life, a family was grieving. I spoke to my therapist Monica a few times while I was in the hospital. Her dad received a double lung transplant at the same time, so she was tending to her own family issues. We talked about the depression and she gave me some meditation techniques to practice. She also insisted that I just continue to send my kidney unconditional LOVE. I needed to "update" him; that he was in a new body now and things were better here. I vowed I wouldn't let this kidney feel that low again. It took some time for me to acknowledge that these dark thoughts were not mine. When they do arise, I send him love instead of going to those dark places with him. It's not easy once your thoughts start to spiral but I reclaimed my control over this body and my thoughts. My therapist and pastor used two different methods of support, but they both wanted me to just relax and trust the universe. Sometimes anxiety can get in the way of your healing. I needed my body to heal and this kidney to know it had a safe, stress-free place to thrive. I needed a name for my kidney. I needed to claim him as mine. He needed to know we're in this together for the long haul. I read the scripture Philippians 4:6 one night, in need of the comfort it always provided me. In that moment the name Phil only made sense. It was perfect. This was his new identity. God knew I needed physical healing and he needed emotional healing and through me we would heal together. Over the next week and a half, things started to improve. I got a better grip on my thoughts, my pneumonia was clearing up, and my hemoglobin levels were holding stable. The plasmapheresis seemed to help but I needed a biopsy of the kidney to confirm it. After reviewing the biopsy, the transplant surgeon noticed there wasn't any reoccurrence of my disease, but it may have suggested another type of disease. He didn't say the name, but typically it is caused by the wrong combination of immunosuppressant drugs. After they switched around some of my medications, the numbers immediately began to stabilize. Each day the numbers kept improving until they were within normal range. Before I was discharged from the hospital I needed one more exit biopsy to fully confirm that there were no signs of reoccurrence. When that biopsy came back normal, I was beyond relieved. Not only was I ready to get out of the hospital after spending two weeks there, post-transplant, but I was ready to get on with the healing process. I knew I still had a few more hurdles before I was in the clear. All of the drains needed to be removed, the staples, the chest catheter, and the old PD catheter—I was sure I would never use it again. Having the PD catheter removed was far more overwhelming than I thought it would be. Coming home and looking in the mirror to find only scars where there had once been tubing was surreal. It signified everything I'd been through and now overcame. All I could say is "My God, you made it." No more dialysis for me. No looking back. Only forward.

Over the next couple of months following a kidney transplant, the transplant team has you come in for blood work and urine tests initially four times a week, then three times, until it tapers down to once a month until you reach the once-a-year milestone. The first year is said to be the hardest because the kidney and your body are still adjusting to each other. I learned that your creatinine (kidney function) will fluctuate and at times I'd worry that my kidney was failing. But every time it went up, it always came back down. I pray to Phil, I continue yoga and meditation, eat healthy and, most importantly, drink lots of water. I CAN'T STRESS ENOUGH HOW IMPORTANT IT IS TO KEEP HYDRATED! The more water you keep flushing through your kidney, the easier it is for it to remove toxins and it doesn't have to work as hard. Once you stop hydrating it, part of the filters begin to die and they won't regenerate. Within the first year is most likely when patients will reject their kidney; so they monitor you closely. Passing the one-year mark is a milestone everyone prays to reach.

TRANSCENDENCE: going beyond the limits of ordinary experience.

I BELIEVE IN LIFE YOU WILL ENCOUNTER roadblocks that seem very detrimental, but when you look back on them they were redirecting you toward a different path. For example, I grew up 100 percent sure I wanted to be a nurse. Then, in high school, I took a deep interest in anesthesiology. So it was settled, I was going to college to receive my Bachelor of Science in Nursing, gain ER experience, and finally apply to Certified Registered Nurse Anesthetist School. I had this whole plan laid out and nothing was going to stop me from achieving this, so I thought. Well, here I am 10 years later, with no degree, no career, and coming up with a new life plan. But now that I look back on it, I can clearly see that my passion for people has always been there, but my path was simply redirected. I was thrown into this community at 19, but I knew I had the power and perseverance to make a difference. The same dedication I would've put toward being the best nurse, I will use to put toward being an even better advocate. The difference is that I simply traded a degree and career for a solid foundation deeply rooted in the renal community. I can always stand on that foundation, no matter what. During my training as a kidney patient peer mentor, I learned that patients diagnosed with chronic illnesses will go through many stages similar to the Stages of Grief, such as Anger, Denial, Bargaining, Depression, Acceptance. Once I finally reached a place of Acceptance of my disease, I then used my story and experience to help others. Beyond Acceptance you move into an even greater stage of Transcendence; which means you utilize all of your extraordinary experience and new outlook on life to impact the lives of others. Once I moved past the self-pity and the what-ifs, I was able to live a more productive and meaningful life. I've accepted this as God's plan for my life and now I can give back to others who haven't reached this stage. I worry many will give up before reaching Transcendence. I didn't think I was going through stages, but now that I reflect over the past eight years, I can clearly map them out. If someone would've told me starting out I would ever live a happy, functional, and productive life as a renal patient, I wouldn't have believed it. I am a renal patient as long as I live. Having a kidney doesn't mean I move on with my life and not reach back to help those still in the fight—or just beginning. I now mentor many men and women by sharing my life experiences and being an example as to what the light at the end of a long very dark tunnel looks like. I am also a member of the Editorial Board of *Kidney Living Magazine* & Peer Mentor (National Kidney Foundation), a member of the Associate Board of the National Kidney Foundation of Illinois, and volunteer with the Healthcare Ministry at my church.

Receiving a kidney transplant feels like having your life restarted. I got my "Do-Over." However, at 22, while on dialysis, I had an epiphany: What if I received my kidney transplant and because I spent basically my whole 20s fighting for my life and not fully doing the things everyone else got to, I started trying to make up for lost time? I never wanted to be the girl acting like a 19-year-old girl in a 27-year-old body. I can tell some areas of my life still need to "grow up." However, I've gained so much wisdom through my trial; mentally I feel much older. When I ran this concern by Monica, she said something that completely shocked me. "She said why not BE THAT GIRL?" Because I have the ability to see the world with child-like eyes, meaning I get to stop and take in the beauty of every little thing. As adults, we get so caught up in "making a living" that we aren't actually "living" anymore. She was so right. I marvel at the smallest things now. Like when a little kid finds so much joy in a lollipop, that's me. I've always felt like a failure, because I never completed college. Until I realized I've completed two things far greater than college to me: five years waiting on a kidney transplant list—and this book.

Made in the USA
Columbia, SC
20 July 2022